Critical Mediur

An honest, critical look at mediumship, scientific evidence and personal experiences

By

Joseph Haigh

Copyright © 2018 Joseph Haigh

All rights reserved, including the right to reproduce this book, or portions thereof in any form. No part of this text may be reproduced, transmitted, downloaded, decompiled, reverse engineered, or stored, in any form or introduced into any information storage and retrieval system, in any form or by any means, whether electronic or mechanical without the express written permission of the author.

ISBN: 978-0-244-96502-0

Thank you's and dedications!

Margaret West:- I dedicate this book to Margaret West, if I had not met you, I doubt I would have stepped back into a Spiritualist Church. I thank you for recognising my potential for development and taking the time to find a teacher who would guide and help me to grow. You are a true spiritualist and a lovely lady.

Helen and Tony Bibby:- I thank you for allowing me to share some great and happy times with you during my development. I will never forget those early days and the fun I experienced. You helped me to openly explore a fascinating world in safe and gentle hands.
Helen, I thank you for teaching the fundamentals: self-discipline, personal responsibility and most of all patience.
Tony, I thank you for the laughs and the time you spent teaching me about energy and how to use this when working with spirit.

Ian Nixon:- I thank you for taking my development to the next level and helping to further understand the mechanics and mechanism to bring about true mediumship. I also thank you for helping me to understand the importance of the process which drives mediumship and what a spiritualist should stand for!!

Caleb, Tillie and Jackson:- This book is no more than my views on a certain subject and I dedicate this book to you. Throughout your lives I encourage you to question and challenge everything with an open mind and with courage, in order to find your own truths which enable you to grow in a loving and graceful way.

Rachael Haigh:- I thank you for supporting me, for all the times you enabled me to grow, develop and follow my passion. I will be forever grateful.

My Guide:- I thank you from the bottom of my heart, for everything.

Introduction

Mediumship has been about for well over 200 hundreds years and the story relating to the Fox sisters is well documented. Historical evidence of purported experiences relating to spiritual encounters have been documented throughout the ages. For me, modern mediumship should be striving for an image that removes the shackles of the darken séance room, the old lady reading tea leaves; mediumship is more than that. Hundreds, if not thousands of psychics/mediums across the country claim they are in communication with higher forces and are somehow enlightened. Yet arguably and rightly so there remains scepticism from critics and the scientific community, who question the validity of such claims and the 'evidence' given in spiritual messages.

It is my genuine belief that this rift between modern mediumship and science should not exist; with further research needed to support a better understanding of human consciousness, and arguably, one of the fundamental questions which has been evident since early mankind - what is after death? There continues to be a huge gap between sceptics and believers alike, with both purporting to have evidence to support their own claims or views, and whilst stand offs between different ideas are nothing new in science and in life, the gap between these two groups continues to grow. There needs to be work undertaken to encourage these groups to come together and begin working in partnership, with barriers and beliefs being broken down, in order to have a resource of evidence both for and against, in which knowledge of our collected purpose can be developed.

It is approximately twelve years ago now that I began to really grasp an understanding of mediumship and its purpose in supporting grieving persons. Up until an encounter with the relatively new show Most Haunted, I had no idea as to what mediums and psychics were, or that a 'chosen few' could make contact with deceased beings. Imagine my surprise and wonder at watching psychic mediums communicating with their 'supposed spirit guides' during the early

2000's, when a boom of television psychic/mediums came to the fore.

Despite my lack of knowledge regarding mediums and psychics, I have always been fascinated with ghosts, supernatural and the unexplained. I remember my family discussing the local ghostly monk, who still made a journey to the local parish church down a chalk lane opposite my house. I remember vividly the many times I sat and played with my Ghostbusters toys and countless viewings of both the films and cartoons. Throughout my life I have always been fascinated with the unexplained and listened in awe when others spoke of their unexplained experiences.

Synchronicity is often referred to within a spiritual context, where events will happen in quick succession and lead to a previously unknown path. In the early 2000's, within a relatively short period of time, I had a number of experiences which led me to visiting a local clairvoyant who advised me that I would end up becoming a spiritualist medium myself! Before visiting said Clairvoyant I had a distinct feeling in my gut that I 'wanted to this', and upon knocking on the door, handing the lady my ring and immediately being told I would develop my own mediumship; I was hooked!

Nearly twelve years on from that initial experience, why decide to write a book on a subject which is arguably widely covered by a number of different authors, from a number of different perspectives. As an individual who is fascinated with mediumship, I know that there must be others out there who feel frustrated, disgruntled and sceptical about teachings and the supposed visions and experiences from so called psychics and mediums across the country. So often I come across statements within books, on websites and on social media which state individuals are communicating with higher forces, or show blurry insect like photo's claiming that scientist refuses to believe the 'evidence' that fairies exist. On a week to week basis, I often view cold reading, vague statements disguised as messages from beyond the grave. Yet there are also times, when I see evidence including names, memories which people can so accurately relate.

Despite believing in a higher force and that the spirit lives on, I also am sceptical and scientific in my thinking. The values and critical thinking which my working practice has helped me to develop, has allowed me to understand and pro-actively reflect on my own mediumship and the quality of the messages I deliver. This book is a collection of thoughts, views and opinions which I have collected over the last few years, in which I hope to answer questions for individuals relating to the teachings from spirit and how they inspire and help people. I will discuss in depth the importance of meditation and how this can aid the quality of mediumship which can be produced. Throughout the book I intend to touch on my own personal experiences to demonstrate the highs, lows and pit falls which can be expected. Finally in the closing sections of the book I will identify examples of modern mediumship which have been tested and present evidence of direct communication with the spirit world.

The book will draw on a number of others resources to help demonstrate that there is positive mediumship, scientific based approaches and good quality evidence for communicating with spirit. This book does not intend to be scientific in nature, more to help promote the interconnection of critical thinking when developing mediumship for the general public and hopefully help critics understand some of the processes and mechanics which underpin good quality spirit communication.

At the time of writing this book, I feel that I am at a place whereby I am able *at times* to provide accurate information including dates, names (both fore and surname) and street names. I consider myself no different to any other medium, and do not see myself as some great mystical person; rather someone who believes that if the spirit world is real, then they should be able to provide accurate and relevant messages.

I hope that this book is used as a tool to support and promote peoples learning, with regard to developing their own mediumship, whilst offering an insight into the highs, lows and at times mind blowing experiences, which can be achieved through hard work, respect and most of all patience. Before we move on to the main contents of this book I want to emphasise that developing mediumship should be a process which enables you to develop compassion, empathy and ultimately a greater sense of yourself in a world full of turmoil, tragedy and globalisation. It is through developing yourself that you become a greater agent for change and recognise the wonders and beauties within this brief existence, and ultimately become a better person. This is what spirituality should be about and of course at times it should be fun too!

Part One: Developing Mediumship

Chapter One: Meditation

The importance of meditation
I can only think of one experience in my childhood, where I may have seen a spirit person, and to this day I am unsure whether what I saw was real, or just someone walking through a field. I remember playing down the same chalk lane, whereby the ghostly monk is reported to roam. On one side of the path there was a railway line and on the other side long flat fields, lying side by side. At the time I was eight years of age and remember my friends and me commenting on a figure walking in the middle of the field, in what appeared to be a long black robe. At that age we thought nothing more, yet looking back, in what only seemed five minutes later, the same individual was in the middle of the next field, bent down. To this day I do not know whether that figure was a spirit, or an eight year olds over active imagination whilst playing whatever game was of interest that day. I mention this story to highlight what I believe to be one of the biggest misconceptions with aspiring mediums; I never saw spirit people when I was growing up. I recall vividly being told by my family that I was always able to find lost items in our house, and people would discuss how intuitive I was. I prefer to think that I was just lucky, rather than having an ability to intuitively perceive where a lost item might be.

Often when attending spiritual groups/events you will come across people who state that they saw spirit growing up, or that they have always sensed spirit people. I am often dubious about such statements, and whilst I am sure *some* mediums have experienced the above, I am also certain that the majority who claim to have seen spirits all their life are saying this because they think it is the right thing to say. I find this sad, partly because they deceive themselves, but also because it is simply not true and this reflects badly upon the wider movement. I like to think that mediumship is like learning an instrument, whilst some might be naturally gifted there are others, myself included, who have had to work hard over time to achieve the same standard.

I think there are a number of fundamental factors which are essential in order to become more spiritual and mediumistic, and one of these is meditation. There are countless different resources which discuss the pros and cons of meditation, which are well worth further exploration, however it is something which at times is arguably not discussed enough with regards to mediumship.

Without meditation as a tool, I would not have been able to develop a mind and the quietness within myself to be able to articulate and give off messages from spirit. Meditation has been the cornerstone of my mediumship and arguably is the single most important tool I have used. This leads me to another experience with which I am regularly confronted. Good quality mediumship takes years to develop and understand, even before you can give accurate and meaningful messages. Yes there are times and exceptions whereby a simple message can strike the very core of an individual, but nine times out of ten, the vagueness of a message leaves people confused, disgruntled and questionable of the power of spirit. It is not uncommon for me to meet someone, who has done a year's development course, who then goes on to charge anywhere from ten pounds upwards for a private reading. The number of times I have come across supposed healers who have done a one or two day course and are supposedly qualified to treat 'patients and ailments'. This in itself is scary as this leaves potentially vulnerable people at risk, believing the person they are seeing is qualified to treat them.

However back to the purpose of meditation, meditation helps to bring relaxation and clarity to your mind, which over time helps you to 'link in' with your own higher spirit being and your spirit guides. It is important to recognise and highlight that your material life always takes priority and realistically you are not always going to be able to meditate on a daily or weekly basis. I raise this as a point, as the art of good meditation is not the length of time you sit, rather the quality and amount of time you have been meditating for. Usually if I have not been able to meditate either due to work commitments or child care, it takes time for me to rebuild that link within myself and then with my higher self and guides.

From experience when using meditation I have found it really helpful to adopt a mindfulness approach. This entails focussing on my natural rhythmic breathing and allowing the mind to become blank. Again I feel that often people expect to meditate a handful of times and then to have direct spirit contact, this is highly unlikely to happen, until you've learnt to let go.

So what do I mean by letting go? To become a medium and give clear accurate messages, you first have to understand yourself. That is what meditation helps you to do, over a period of time it allows for you to work through all that 'emotional baggage' which you've unconsciously collected throughout your life. Once you begin this journey through meditation you will begin to notice changes in your everyday life, you become calmer, less anxious and begin to develop compassion for yourself and others.

Over the last year, I have really started to strip back my meditations; no longer do I need music, numerous candles and everything to be 'right'. Meditation should be a process whereby you can sit, contemplate and be at one with yourself, regardless of where you are. In the early days I did use calm music whenever I meditated and there is nothing wrong with this, as it helps you keep focussed, and gives you an idea of how long you have been meditating and this is helpful, especially when just starting out. As you become more accustomed to meditation and you develop it as a skill, the need to hold on to rituals gradually changes and you recognise the need to let go of thoughts, materialistic items and appreciate the moment whilst practising. Having said this, I still find it important to have the following items, a comfy chair (I like the support a single futon chair gives me), my piece of amethyst crystal (sometimes rose quartz for healing) and a single candle. The reason I have these items is because they help my mind to focus and recognise that I want to have quiet time to reflect and process my thoughts along with the ups and downs of everyday life. Having said this I now utilise meditation in everyday life including times when I focus on my breathing in meetings at work to help my mind focus.

- **My recommendations for meditating:**

Ever since I met my first spiritual teachers, Helen and Tony Bibby, the importance of meditation has been stressed to me. It is important for me to mention at this point and prior to telling this story, that I have had some mind-blowing experiences, some which I genuinely cannot explain. Whilst I mentioned earlier in the book that it is unlikely you would experience spirit contact almost straight away, sometimes this does happen. This is exactly what happened to me during the first ever meditation I had, however I stress that experiences such as the one I am about to discuss have been few and far between. I believe when I get experiences like this the purpose is to direct me, or make me aware of a new teaching. As I have progressed through my spiritual journey, the experiences have started to cluster together and occur on a more regularly basis. I think this is happening due to the amount of spiritual work and meditation I am currently doing, especially as I have finished full time education and my babies begin to sleep through the night……..mostly!

During the first evening I started on my spiritual journey, it was focussed predominantly on getting to know each other and ascertaining what direction I wanted to take my developing mediumship. From early on I realised that I wanted to demonstrate in local churches on the rostrum and if I recall correctly this is the response I gave to Helen and Tony. During that evening I was informed that we would try a short meditation to see how I fared. During this process I listened to Helen's voice and was helped into a calm and relaxing meditation, nothing more. However as I sat and questioned whether I was actually doing it right I began to feel as though I was lifting, not physically lifting, rather my 'being' lifting and pulling towards the front right of me. At this point I saw two blurry and golden-light figures standing in front of me, a vision I had never seen before or since. It was such a bizarre experience and left me confused and unsure what I had seen, even thinking about it know brings the butterflies back in my stomach. When coming out of the meditation I remember Tony and Helen smiling and checking to see if I was okay. The first thing they said was: 'you saw something, didn't you?' I explained what had occurred and both took time to explain the experience to me, even if I think they were a little surprised that I had already experienced something. I think the reason for not experiencing something like that since is because I have held onto that experience and began to build barriers in how I think mediumship should work. Although sad, it is common for people to build barriers in the mind and part of the process of development is using a tool such as meditation, to help break down those barriers and help to remove preconceived expectations.

So why meditate, what is its purpose in helping your mediumship? Meditation helps to quiet the mind, helps to bring focus and allows a process for dealing with your emotional baggage. Once you start this process, it is at this point that you can begin linking with spirit on a deeper level. Gordon Smith discusses the importance of recognising your own spirit and the need to link into this as well as recognising there may be wider spiritual beings guiding and directing you. It seems daft to me, but so many people are desperate to make contact with spirit beings that they completely disregard understanding their own spirit being! How sad, that someone has the opportunity to connect with themselves on a deeper level and they neglect it in the hope of achieving more. Meditation is the fundamental driving force behind good mediumship and the other factors associated with it, including healing. Understanding this basic tool and utilising it on a regular basis will enable you to achieve stronger and more accurate messages as a medium in the longer term. To this very day I would argue that it is the single most important technique I have used to develop my mediumship and I doubt I would be at the level I am now without it.

My top tips for meditation:

1) Make sure you are not full up from lunch/tea etc. This can impact on your experience and become uncomfortable and essentially put you off. Often I will try to meditate before my tea, to

ensure that I can relax and not worry about having to meditate afterwards.

2) Posture/sitting right. I personally struggle to meditate if my back is not straight. There are a number of reasons for keeping a straight back, including keeping a good posture and supporting effective breathing. Find what is comfortable and works for you, but try to ensure that blood flow and circulation are not obstructed causing discomfort including pins and needles etc. Often you will see pictures of people sat on a cushion with their legs folded, personally this doesn't work for me, but if you find it comfortable then use that method.

3) Short and sweet, then build up. Initially it will be hard to achieve a state of meditation which is sustained were you can achieve a state of true mindfulness. My advice is to start with shorter meditations; maybe five minutes a day then build up gradually. Guided meditations, such as the ones provided by Gordon Smith are excellent for beginners.

4) Breathing. This is arguably the most important factor when meditating, as it is the key to achieving a mindfulness state. Slow deep regular breaths help to bring calm, relaxation and focus to a meditation. This can then be used and put into practice in everyday life. It is important to ensure that you use the whole of your lung capacity and this can be monitored by observing your stomach motion moving up and down. After a while, you can use this technique to help calm you when you are in situations which naturally build anxiety such as job interviews etc.

It can be difficult to stop your mind wandering off, or a thought pop into your mind and then become fixated on this or the emotion which it makes you feel. The purpose of mindfulness is to be aware, acknowledge that thought and let it pass out of your conscious awareness. This is the benefit of observing your breathing as it helps to focus the mind back on meditating. When I have previously led meditation sessions for groups they have often commented stating that I 'knew when' to bring their mind to focus on their breathing. My explanation wasn't that I was aware of their energies or spiritually attuned to their energy more my own personal experiences of meditation and my own mind wandering.

Further tips for meditation include using soft music, creating a quiet space and using guided meditations. It is what works for you and there should be no hard and fast rules about how you achieve a meditative state of mind. If you are struggling to manage meditation by yourself, try group meditations, or researching different techniques. A good spiritualist church will have some advice/guidance on meditation or classes which are available in your local area. Often an excellent place to get information on meditative practices is a local Buddhist centre and arguably they are master of such practices.

It is important to highlight another frustration I have found during development; the need for people to drift off to 'apparent' faraway dimensions and see wonderful and mystical things. Have you ever been in a group and felt saddened or sceptical about another member's experience? There is nothing wrong with asking for evidence or clarity of what that person saw, they may have travelled to these places, but I would ask whether their experience was supernatural or a visualisation within their own mind. For any developing mediums, in circles already, it is important to recognise the role of a group leader when partaking in a meditation class. The leader needs to remain focussed and ensure that the groups energies are blending and that everyone is being supported to experience and achieve a state of mindfulness. Again, if your teacher is travelling to mystical places every week I would ask what is the purpose of this, is it spirit or their way of having the focus on them?! Don't get me wrong, visualised meditations can be a good way to bring mindfulness or be taken on a journey to help you reflect on different aspects of your life, but they need to be used in conjunction with regular meditation to ensure a good equal balance to your overall practice.

It is worth using a pen and note pad to make sure you document your experiences, it is surprising how you begin to notice patterns and different feelings over the course of time and you never know they may help you further on in your development.

As you begin to develop regular meditation, you of course will begin to notice changes, both within yourself and how you perceive the world. I remember when I had started meditating on a regular basis I noticed a number of changes. In my early twenties I was angry and had a 'short fuse', I genuinely noticed that I became calmer and able to deal with things differently. Nowadays I use meditation to help me bring focus to my day to day challenges whether that is anxiety, worry or stress relating to work, or to help my general overall health and well-being. Meditation is not only a tool for connecting to the higher self, it should be a process where you learn to become less reactive to situations and more reflective, acting with compassion, kindness and a calm mind.

I have definitely noticed a number of differences relating to my spiritual awareness using meditation. During my time working as a mechanic, I remember being at the top of a 'cherry picker'/platform machine undertaking some checks. As part of doing this I use to love looking at the surrounding fields and the near sea wall. During this time I noticed the long grass in the field next to me swaying from side to side which focused my mind. At this point I felt a connectedness to all that was around me and felt at one. It was a beautiful moment which I think will stay with me for a number of years to come. Another change I notice particularly when I begin meditating, when I have not had opportunity to for a while, is the clarity of my vision. I often notice this when I am out in nature walking my dogs, I call it my 'HD vision' as everything around me appears clearer and more defined. Furthermore, I become more aware of things around me, no longer is my mind busy moving from one thought to the next, rather I allow myself to appreciate the sound birds make, the wonderful colours nature produces and the beautiful night sky. It is so easy in today's society to lose focus and become fixated on the must have must-have gadgets or alternatively the issue for that particular day. I often think about the Buddhist monks and how reflective and calm they look, even when faced with adversity. Often Buddhist monks lead lives which are stripped back and have an understanding of the need to be reflective and consider the positives and remain in the here and now.

So meditation can have a wonderful effect not only on your mediumship but also your everyday life and I suspect over the next ten years meditation will enter more in the general public attention and hopefully be promoted as a preventative measure to general anxiety disorders which are common place in today's society.

So within the initial stages of this book, we have briefly gone over a number of fundamental elements which can help you grow and develop as a medium. Remember it takes time however it is time well spent. Even if you decide that spiritualism is not for you, meditation should help you to learn more about yourself, as a person and develop compassion for others. Remember it would be good if you can develop these skills in a group setting, however meditation and spiritual development can be done independently, in the enjoyment of your own home.

Sensing spirit: Chapter Two

The differences between meditation and moving to noticing spirit interaction:
Whilst you start to process and change your life through meditation, you are also giving yourself opportunity to feel and sense energies which are constantly around you. When sat in the silence of your own being and you have started the process of clearing your thoughts, it's at this point that you may start to become more aware of the subtle changes going on in and around your body. Initially you're going to begin to feel what your body does every day unconsciously, including breathing rhythm and heartbeat, take time to appreciate this. Recognise how your body feels in this state so you don't confuse this with other experiences you may have later on.

Next you're likely to begin feeling your own energy field and overtime this may go from awareness of your own bodily functions through to beginning to feel slight vibrations, more intense heart beat and some perceived expansion of self. I would say that most people get confused at this point; including me originally when I believed it to be other spirits, and it is probably a really common mistake. This is a really important aspect to grasp, it is spirit; your spirit! So many people overlook this fundamental point, because they want to connect to higher spirits, guides etc. Gordon Smith highlights that most guide's principle purpose is to guide you, to you. I think this is a really interest concept and it has certainly helped me to recognise the different levels when developing. Understanding your own spirit and listening to what it is trying to tell you, not only in development but in life, is such an important aspect of development. Learn from it and continue to grow, it is likely that these initial experiences may feel intense and my take time to process, however this is definitely not an issue through development.

I suppose it could be argued that I have a conflict of interest, with science, by believing there are wider forces which I connect with to pass information on from deceased relatives. Actually, what I would say is that I am open minded and reflective about the experiences I and others have. Of course, not every single unexplained phenomenon is paranormal in nature, nor is it explained away by our current understandings of science. This is highlighted within aspects of social science, including psychology, whereby a professional may offer their interpretation on a behaviour or nature, rather than being able to scientifically measure and repeat that test. Having said that, just because science cannot explain something only interpret, it does not mean it is paranormal in nature.

This is a really important point to grasp and something which I feel often frustrates scientist when researching the paranormal. People will hide behind and use aspects of science to back up their claims when clearly there are often none or very abstract links between them. A good example is quantum physics, whereby the general public have a misinterpreted view about what quantum physics is and its applications and then use it to interpret and justify their mediumship. So, as far as I am aware, quantum healing has not been tested and proved within laboratories and no medium/scientist so far has offered an article to a peer review journal regarding this subject.

Thus back to my original train of thought, when I use the word 'energy' I use it to describe the things I feel around me when I sense spirit. I use the word energy as a general term, as everything around us including ourselves can be classed as an energy force. It is important to keep the terminology used as simplistic as this and not try and put a misconceived perception using pseudo-science.

So let us recap on the above. Remember to take time to process these initial experiences, the more time taken to do this in the beginning will inevitably help you progress in the longer term. I love sitting in open circles, or within private groups, and seeing people develop and see the genuineness and compassion in what they are conveying. I'd rather listen to that, than someone who is focussed on what they are experiencing and getting caught up in thinking something is spiritual when it is not. Please don't get me wrong, I do think everyone experiences sensations which they perceive are some higher being rather than self; however there becomes a point whereby as a student you should begin to recognise the different levels and move past these experiences.

The auric field

When beginning to sense energies around you and connecting with others, it is important to understand other aspects of what you might perceive. Initially you are likely to sense your own being, which then moves on to having a greater awareness of energies around you and then your own aura. If I am being honest my knowledge of the aura and how to fully utilise it within readings is still developing. What I can tell you is that everything has some form of aura, including to a certain extent, inanimate objects. There are numerous techniques to see the aura, and I usually see it more prominently when someone is stood in front of a white background. The aura is the energy field an object is giving off, and can be used by psychics and mediums to pick out information about what is happened or going on in a person's life. Quite often when I am working or sat not really paying attention, I will notice a faint glow around an individual's shoulders and head area. One thing I have learnt when undertaking readings is that sometimes I will glimpse a colour around a person and these colours usually signify specific prompts. When I see the colour green in someone's aura this often means that person has a caring/nursing background, or alternatively the colour blue, dependent upon where I see it, either means that the person is a natural healer or they are currently receiving healing from spirit.

Sensing the aura

If you are part of a group or even developing by yourself, try and experiment feeling others energies including their aura. My advice would be to do the following:

1)   Stand behind a person who is sat in a chair
2)   Relax and place your hands on their shoulders
3)   Begin to relax yourself through your breathing and take yourself into a state whereby you are able to sense
4)   Once in this state focus on your hands and see if you can sense a difference in the vibrational state compared to yours. Does it

feel fast, warm, and/or strong? You may even pick up thoughts, health issues or worries that person is feeling.

5) Try moving your hands slightly above the shoulders and move around that area does it feel different?

6) Once you have done this, relax and chat and share experiences. Don't get disheartened if you feel nothing, it can take time to develop awareness of more subtle energies and it is more important to be honest with yourself and others, rather than to deceive yourself.

This is a really good exercise for students to practise and try on a regular basis, as it helps to develop awareness of subtle energies which eventually you will adopt when doing readings. Remember to reflect and discuss with others your experiences and don't be afraid to ask questions of your teacher! A good teacher should help *you* to identify reflective questions for what you have experienced not simply give you the answer.

It is important to discuss how the aura can be used within a reading; often the aura and energies around an individual are used by psychics to pick up information. This is an important distinction between a medium and psychic whereby a medium goes beyond that auric field and energy around a person and connects to spirit. Often I will hear people talk about visiting a psychic and actually it sounds as though they have had a mixture of psychic and spiritual reading. It depends what you're after from a reading, however a good psychic or medium will give you a reading that heals and helps to answers questions you may have. This is a really interesting point and is a subject often spoke spoken about in the circle I currently sit in. My current teacher made a decision not to do private readings, as often the people he saw were more interested in their future rather than receiving a message from a loved one. It is important to distinguish between the four different types of readings a person is likely to experience:

1) Fortune Reading- used to tell people if they are going to get the man, job, car, house whatever they're after for the future. Whilst I do not judge future tellers per se, it's not something which I am interested in doing.

2) Psychic- A reading whereby an individual will read your aura/energies around you and tell you what has been happening around you recently and what *may happen* in your near future. Often psychics will be able to pick on potential routes and pathways which are already pre-determined to a certain exact and are showing what paths you may take

3) Mediumship/spiritual – This is used to bring a connection from a passed relative/friend and to prove life continues hereafter. Furthermore a reading should enable an opportunity for connection through love with a person on the other side and help to bring closure as part of a grieving process and bring healing to that person. Predominantly this is my area of interest and where I currently do the majority of my readings.

4) Mediumship/psychic- Often you will see individuals advertised as 'psychic mediums', which simply means they use both mediumistic and psychic tools in a reading process. This is something which I am slowly developing and incorporating into my readings.

I feel it is important to explain these differences not only to the novice but also to people further on in their development as this is not *always* explained to the student, thus they become confused about what tools they are using.

I thought it would be good to discuss Aura photography and how this can be used to see the different colours around the individual. It is a number of years since I last had a photo of my aura taken, purely due to the fact I currently do not feel it necessary. I remember when I was training and my teacher Helen used to speak about a Red Indian guide who worked with her called White Cloud. Whilst talking about Aura photography, Helen told me a story about how White Cloud had shown himself to her in an aura photograph laughing. When Helen asked why he was laughing, he simply explained that it was in response to his beliefs whilst alive that a camera could steal a person's soul. Well, as you can imagine, the thought of seeing a spirit person caught on film in such a way was really exciting to me, and upon seeing the photo a number of months later, a laughing face of a guide could be clearly seen next to Helen's face. It is rare to see such pictures, and if truth be told, I would love to view it again and perhaps have it analysed to help ensure it is not a trick of the light or a focus issue on the camera lens.

It is important to recognise how to sense energy and aura's as this will no doubt help you to bring clearer and more defined readings to others when working with them. If in a development group, or even developing on your own it is helpful to talk to others about your experiences and to help you try and understand what is going on and why you are experiencing what you are feeling, seeing and sometimes hearing. Where possible I would encourage others to work within a group setting, however it's not always the only way. Throughout my development, initially I sat within a group which over time twiddled off and despite wanting to I could not find a local group, thus I began to meditate by myself and use books to help gain knowledge. It is only now that I am back within a development group, and understand that actually spirit wanted me to develop independently and this worked for me.

Chakras

The topics discussed in this book are my opinions of what mediumship is and how it should be developed, however there are various ways in which mediums develop and equally various tools used. The purpose of this book is to demystify elements of development, take some of the 'silliness' out of it and provide a structure which often is sadly lacking. I want it to be based in some fact and evidence based which you can further explore.

I want to briefly discuss Chakras and how they help me to work with spirit and also bring balance to my life. This is one of the areas in the book whereby I cannot provide evidence of their existence; only going off my own experiences during my development and how they have had a positive impact.

Throughout my early development I was taught about these energy centres situated within the human body which when not aligned or balanced can impact on our daily life. Chakras as I learnt to call them derive from Indian cultures and often are associated with Hinduism and elements of Tibetan Buddhism. They are described as subtle energy centres all over the body which interact with the higher self and when these energy centres are not aligned, or blocked they can have an effect on the physical self, such as making the individual feel lethargic, or alternatively contributing to a feeling of disconnection.

Chakras are reported to be throughout the human body; however there is a general consensus that the main seven which run vertically through the centre of the human body are the most important ones. In a spiritual context aligning these Chakras and balancing them can contribute towards greater health and wellbeing whilst also strengthening the connection with your higher self and the spirit realms. The third eye (located in the middle of the forehead) is often described by mediums/psychics as a tool for sensing the unseen world, helping them deliver messages to recipients and is one of the main seven Chakras.

Initially I was sceptical about these spheres of unseen energy, even thinking to myself 'well they've never needed aligning before, so why start now!' Furthermore I was frustrated that I could apparently sense these energy centres yet when I tried I felt nothing. As I developed early on, the importance of closing down my third eye and other Chakras was drummed into me to ensure that the physical and spiritual part of my life remained separate. As a result I continued to think about Chakras and try to understand their purpose and impact on my spiritual development.

In 2008 I visited Cornwall with my family and came across an alternative spiritual shop near Bude and found a Chakra cleansing C.D which I ended up purchasing. Initially cautious I decided to give the 45 minute meditation a try and throughout was asked to focus energy from spirit through the top of my head and begin to visualise these energy centres cleansing and building them in strength. During the meditation I struggled to follow the strong visualisations and afterwards did not really feel much different, or 'spiritually cleansed'. However after a while I noticed that I seemed to be more in tune and my mind was more clear and calm. This was further confirmed when I was sat at work later that day listening to the general conversation and recall someone being asked their middle name. At this point I can only describe a visualisation where I saw the name Louise suddenly pop up in my mind's eye in front of the individual in question and was even more surprised when she stated her middle name was in fact Louise.

Since that time I have taken time out to focus and cleanse my Chakras on a regular basis whilst also trying to learn more about them. I believe the seven main Chakras play a vital role in my spiritual development and also have a positive impact on everyday life and my emotional wellbeing. After working spiritually I use to practise closing my third eye and main chakras down, which allowed me to focus on everyday life, which I still use to this day. However it is important to note that I do not physically close these down more the fact I am acknowledging to myself that I am no longer linking into spirit.

Recently in church I had an experience whereby I linked with spirit and visualised energy entering through the top of my head into my Chakras. At this point I experienced increased vibrations within my body and felt spirit step extremely close almost to the point I felt would enter a trance state (to be discussed later). This further has confirmed the power and use of Chakras and their importance in development. Interestingly a member of the public commented that whilst I was meditating she could see energies building around me with crystals surrounding me, which again affirmed the experience. This was interesting particularly as I normally don't have experience like that on a regular basis, nor had people comment, saying they see such things around me when in church.

The seven Chakras run straight down the human body with the Crown Chakra being situated above the top of the head and the base Chakra being situated at the base of the coccyx bone. When I visualise them, I see them in my mind's eye as large spheres which sit in my body spinning and each have their own size and colour. It is important to mention that I doubt they are actually like that, however that is my own way of feeling and sensing of them, and others may feel them differently. Don't worry if you struggle with visualisations, seeing things is one of the biggest areas where I struggle. My advice is to learn to feel and sense rather than see things as in the long term this will no doubt benefit you more.

So let us have a look at the individual Chakra and what they represent including the colours and how they interact with both your spiritual and physical life. Given the role some Chakras play in spiritual work, it is easy to focus on one or two but be wary taking this approach, I would argue that they have equal importance in bringing balance and contributing towards spirit development.

Crown Chakra –
Where: Above your head
Colours: Violet

Spiritual Purpose: The Crown Chakra is seen as your link to spirit, to the wider consciousness and to the universe. Often practitioners will visualise this as the point which the physical and spiritual connect when working with the spirit world. When opening up to work with spirit, often I will imagine white light entering my body through the Crown Chakra and subsequently through the rest of my body.

Physical Benefits: Often associated with developing insight and intellect on deeper level, often associated with a philosophical perspective.

Third Eye/pineal Gland –
Where: In the middle of your forehead
Colour: Indigo

Spiritual Purpose: *for seeing*, the Third eye is where you may get clairvoyant and psychic visions often associated with sensing the unseen world. I believe that both the crown and third eye Chakra when utilised together are extremely helpful in linking with spirit and working in a spiritual way.

Physical benefits: Allows you to develop better intuition and knowing, whilst also enabling you to sense when things are not right. An example could be 'knowing' when the phone is going to ring, or being able to anticipate things better in everyday life. A further physical benefit is the likelihood of reduce headaches and your reaction to stress is likely to reduce too.

Throat Chakra –
Where: In your throat
Colour: Blue

Spiritual Purpose: To be able to communicate from spirit effectively and more clearly, allowing you to speak clearer the word of spirit. I would suggest that when working clairsentient or clairaudient this Chakra allows that communication to be clearer and less interrelated with your own thoughts as an individual. Furthermore when communicating with people in your everyday life, it allows you to communicate more effectively your feelings and understand others as well.

Physical benefits: By balancing the energy in the throat Chakra you are likely to experience less colds and sore throats and better sinuses.

Heart Chakra –
Where: In the region near your heart
Colour: Green

Spiritual Purpose: To love, heal and show compassion it is that simple! By balancing the energy in the Heart Chakra you are developing all of the above and you will notice this both in your daily and spiritual life. The messages you deliver as a result of this Chakra will be more compassionate and allow you to bring love and guidance through from spirit. It should also allow you to manage your emotions when delivering messages in general, as at times it can be emotional connecting loved ones.

Physical benefits: Firstly you will notice you are less reactive towards others and situations, developing a deeper level of compassion, whilst also noticing a greater balance in your own emotional state. Secondly you are likely to experience less heart pain and heart burn etc.

Solar Plexus Chakra –
Where: Around your belly button
Colour: Yellow

Purpose: Whilst all have equal importance, I would suggest this one is very important in providing energy and by balancing this Chakra it enables you to have more energy both in a spiritual and physical sense developing vitality and desire to do things. This Chakra is important when delivering spiritual messages as it enables you to sustain a standard, acting as a battery pack, thus it is imperative to sustain and cleanse regularly.

Physical Benefits: With this Chakra you are likely to be more committed to completing things and more driven in your everyday life. You are likely to experience fewer issues with the stomach area and bowels.

Sacral Chakra –
Where: Just above your genital area
Colour: Orange
Purpose: This Chakra allows you to have greater emotional regulation both in your messages and everyday life. By balancing this Chakra it enables you to have deeper understanding of your emotions and use them in a positive way.

Physical Benefits: The physical benefits of utilising this Chakra are better sexual productivity, and greater control of your emotional state relating to relationships.

Base Chakra –
Where: Located near the Coccyx
Colour: Red
Purpose: Ground and stability. The bottom Chakra a deep red colour, one which grounds you in a spiritual context ensuring that you do not become too 'airy fairy' in your development, and help you recognise the need to be balanced between the physical and spiritual self.

Physical Benefits: Overall greater grounding in life can be achieved with this Chakra ensuring that you recognise your longer term commitments.

On a very basic level, this is what Chakras are and plenty of information regarding them can be found on the internet. Remember keep it simple, and once you feel able to sense (energies) around you, then you can begin to sense the subtle energy of the different Chakras. Developing a simple visualisation will help you in practices relating to balancing your Chakras if and when required.

A 'simple technique'…..

When I am meditating and I want to balance/cleanse my Chakras I focus on them, their position and colour and visualise them spinning and focus on their vibrancy. I then ask my guides to allow white light to enter my Crown Chakra and as this happens I visualise the light cleansing that individual Chakra making it brighter, stronger and aligned within my body. Once I feel this is complete I visualise that energy going through my other Chakras and leaving my body. I continue to do to this for each individual Chakra and ensure that they are vibrant, Strong and aligned. This is quite a complex feat to achieve and may take time to be able to do, and my advice regarding this would be to try and find a sensible teacher who can guide you through this process until you feel able to complete yourself.

Unfortunately as stated previously I cannot provide evidence that Chakras exist, although the impact they have had on my everyday life and spiritual work cannot be ignored. Whilst I am unable to demonstrate in a scientific manner they exist, I feel it is important to discuss in line with on-going spiritual development. A final thought on Chakras, my advice would be to undertake an exercise at least once a month whereby you visualise your Chakras and cleanse them.

Moving on from the psychic levels, through to sensing spirit and others

I thought I would share an experience I had in the earlier years of my development and (peoples') perspectives. I remember commenting on a Facebook status regarding my mediumship and stating that I was still developing and a lady responded stating that mediums do not develop, they are born. When reading that comment I became frustrated, deleted my own comments and felt foolish, as people didn't agree with what I had stated. I raise this as a discussion point to remind people that it is okay to have your own views on mediumship, as long as they are true to yourself. As time has gone by I no longer associate with online discussions regarding spiritualism and ghost, etc, as often it ends with people being rude, or alternatively closed minded in their opinion. On the opposite of this, I've genuinely become disillusioned with other people who think everything that EVER happens is spiritual in nature. I suppose I should make my views very clear: Fairies and Dragons are fairy-tale stuff and not the subject of true mediumship and genuine psychical phenomenon.

Whilst it is up to you to formulate your own views and opinions, I think it is helpful to base your mediumship on your own experiences and beliefs, whilst also reading literature which is sensible and/or fact based. By doing this, it helps to put context to your beliefs and also helps to keep a balanced approach. This is one of the reasons I feel that mediumship should have some scientific basis whilst also remembering that it requires an artistic nature to deliver, which is something which that will be discussed in more depth at a later stage in the book.

Moving between sensing energy/auras to beginning to sense spirits

Rightly so you may state, I have experienced spirit beings well before this point and often get messages for others; or alternatively you may be feeling frustrated at the lack of consistency when you are able to sense spirit or the lack of spirit interaction you've achieved compared to your peers!

The purpose of writing this section is to highlight the need to develop tools and skills to experience controlled and intentional spirit interaction. I think it is really important to develop these skills to ensure that if you experience spirit interaction it is achieved through choice, control and more importantly when required. I ask you to think and reflect on this point: *What purpose does it serve, to continually be having interactions with the spirit world?* Whose purpose does this serve if you're not helping others, what does it prove and to whom? Whilst it may be reassuring, it is not healthy to continually be open to the spirit world. I often come across people who say *'I am always open to spirit'* or *'I can't close down'*. I would personally say that is more about their own personal responsibility and choice. I can honestly say that, there are times I go for days without meditating and then *'lose'* that spiritual connection, or alternatively can meditate and control the ability to have spirit connections. Don't get me wrong there are times, when I have been working and noticed spirit or alternatively got a 'feeling' when meeting someone or seeing something, but this is glancing and goes as soon as it appeared. The medium Gordon Smith speaks about the need to lead a physical life, as well as a spiritual life and the need to ground yourself in reality. I think this is a really important point to grasp, especially early on, so you don't become too big headed or believe every situation in your life should be a spiritual experience. So in short, don't be that person who tells everyone you're always open to spirit! It doesn't make you look any better and in the short term might get you some attention, but inevitably won't bring greater spirituality.

It is important to understand the difference between seeing, sensing and hearing spirit. It is imperative to understand those subtler energies surrounding you and how this works with your other sense such as sight, hearing, emotions etc and this is where meditation is used to help build these links. Mediumship is a build-up of many different layers and learning the difference between them and how to navigate will always take time, patience and practice. Recognising that a deeper level of clarity and understanding can be gained by sensing as well as seeing will improve your communication during a reading. I used to get frustrated and ask spirit to 'show themselves' and then I would have concrete confirmation of their existence and it took me a long time to appreciate the need to learn the language of spirit and use all my senses. Think about it, if you were a spirit person and wanted to show someone how much you loved them, would it be easier to express that visually, or by giving the medium a feeling of love, probably one that she/he will recognise instantly. Alternatively if a spirit person is trying to show you they had really bad knee pain, would it be more helpful for them to dance on around hopping up and down on one leg, or allow the medium to feel what they felt? I believe this evidences well the reason why it takes a medium so long to develop, because you have to learn these deeper levels of understanding and work to use them simultaneously. Working with spirit is more than just seeing them stood there. Utilising all your senses, to communicate and relate messages, is hard but the rewards are well worth it.

Just a final note on the need to learn how to sense spirit, I remember in the early days when I was just learning I remember being sat in open circle and getting the strong sensation that I had been hit round the back of the head with a bat and I recall seeing a faint vision with this of a man with a bat. I played it off because it sounded so bizarre and realistically in a room full of 40 people what would be the chances of someone knowing a person being killed in such a way? As a result of my doubt, I brushed these thoughts away and continued enjoying the evening, it was only later on when the lady sat next to me started describing what I had seen and I was stunned. I often know now that spirits are around me, or I had a spiritual experience because the hairs on my arm go tingly. Learning to sense as well as see is fundamental in your quest to be a good rounded medium.

So let us reflect:
By using meditation this helps to clear your mind and allow for emotional baggage to be processed whilst also allowing you to become more aware of the subtler energies around you. At this point you can then begin to sense the aura, Chakras and other people's energies. Overtime as you begin to recognise the differences you then should begin to experience the sensations of spirit and what they are trying to communicate with you. By using meditation you allow your mind to become clearer and allow the messages to come through in a purer fashion and with less interpretation from your own values and perspectives.

I would say everyone has their own way of working with spirit using different techniques and approaches to sensing, hearing and seeing. A good example of this would be to get each of the group to visualise a simple object like an orange. Each person in the group will likely have different ways of visualising the orange, with some being more vivid and real whilst perhaps others view it as more faded or perhaps look like a cartoon orange. The point being, that everyone experiences things in a different way and in a different context, like when I do this exercise I will often focus on the peel and the lines upon it however this will be faint and hard to see. I sometimes wonder if this is one of the reasons for supposed errors or mix ups when a medium gives a reading and there are slight inaccuracies; remember everyone sees things differently and if a spirit personality is trying to communicate what an orange looks like, the medium may be focussing on a different aspect of the orange rather than the skin, if (the medium) is looking at the segments instead. This is perhaps why aspects of readings get confused when a medium is trying to describe a feeling or alternatively trying to decipher something which the spirit personality has shown them in his/her mind.

It would be good to discuss further at this point the different ways a spirit personality may influence the energies around you to communicate. It is well written about the general types of spirit communication and I do not feel it is appropriate to rewrite in-depth about these here and other books are available and I recommend doing more research on these topics.

The three main areas are:

1) Clairsentient: This is where the medium will often sense the spirit in that the spirit personality will manipulate the energies around the medium to make them aware of their presence. Alternatively the spirit person may allow the medium to feel an illness, perhaps a beard/long hair or a distinctive feature.

2) Clairaudient: This is where a medium may hear the spirit voice, hear music or alternatively hear a distinctive sound relating to the individual. I think often mediums get confused with this way of perceiving spirit and believe they will hear the spirit voice directly. Whilst that is probably true for some, for me I tend to hear my own voice and this is usually the words of the spirit personality. It can be difficult to tell the difference at first, however over time this becomes easier as you sense those light vibrational changes around you when spirit step near.

3) Clairvoyant: This is by far the most well-known way of working with spirits and many claim to be clairvoyant. Alternatively at times genuine mediums may use it as umbrella term to highlight their skills. There is a common misconception with regards to how people believe they will see spirit people. Yes there may be times when you see a fully materialised spirit personality but for me these incidents are rare and often fleeting visions. Often when I am

working I will see an image in my mind eyes, or alternatively get a glimpse of an image next to someone. When out and about and on those rare occasions I might see a spirit individual this is when I tend to see a full materialisation, however these images are fleeting and tend to be out the corner of my eye.

I think people get confused over how they should work and I regularly hear people state *'I'm Clairvoyant'*, or *'I'm Clairsentient/I hear spirit'*. I remember this well and desperately wanted to see spirit, however overtime I began to realise and understand that spirit tried to communicate with me predominantly through sense. Upon realising this and using it I began to believe that I was a Clairsentient, however what I now know is I use a combination of all three and upon realising this my mediumship started to flow more easily. Whilst you may have one sense which is 'stronger' than others, don't let that define you as a medium, in fact I urge you to do the opposite. By not putting barriers up, you enable yourself to be utilised by spirit in a whole host of different ways which over time will increase your accuracy during readings.

Imagine a spirit person is stood in front of you and you can describe them down to a tee, that's great. But imagine if you solely focus on developing this skill, how would spirit then be able to show you how they felt, or tell you a phrase, a name that would provide that absolute proof? Unfortunately when clairvoyant, spirits don't come with flip chart and pens to write down messages to pass on, nor do they practice mime techniques to describe feelings. When I am reading for an individual I may feel a sensation letting me know that a person died in an accident, or I may visually see them holding a sentimental piece of jewellery or I might hear a special piece of music, word or phrase which the sitter can relate too. Allow yourself to become open to allowing spirit to interact with you in different ways and you will be surprised at what they can do. If you do hear someone stating they are this or that, just acknowledge it and let it go, usually these are the ones that are either self-proclaimed or have little understanding of the mechanics behind good quality mediumship.

Don't worry if this seems a lot to take in or try to remember. My advice would be to focus on clearing your mind by meditating and just be aware. Take yourself through the meditation, then become aware of your energies and the wider energies around, but try and do this without focusing too much or straining to get a message. Allow it to be a natural process and see what happens, you never know you might just get that vital piece of evidence.

Hopefully as a developing medium you will have a good teacher and practice opportunities within a group setting; if you don't have these don't worry! Use good resources available to you and trust your instincts. Later on in the book I will focus on other mediums already accomplished whom I believe provide a sound platform for helping any developing medium to grow and develop. A technique I have found helpful over the years includes developing reflection, which is a technique to help you rationalise and think back on your experiences ; again this is usually useful within a group setting but equally can be used independently. There will no doubt be times whereby you get things wrong, you get frustrated at the lack of clarity or progress you're making. Use both meditation and reflection to help understand why you are at that point in your development. Maybe you have to focus on material things happening in your life, or are you missing important aspects of development or a particular teaching at that point? The whole process can takes years to go through but it is worth the wait and you will notice the difference in your mediumship.

Guides: Chapter Three

Guides, who they are, and what their purpose is?

It is perhaps relevant to discuss guides at this point and how they can aid your continual development. I have two guides whom work with me. The first being a gentleman I met quite early on in my development. I remember sitting on my bed meditating one day when all of a sudden, I became aware of a man's head rotating in my mind's eye. This was unusual for me as my ability to visualise clearly in my head is quite poor, yet this vision was clear and fixed in its characteristics. I released at that point that I was seeing my guide and since then to my knowledge I have never seen his face like that again, only seeing an outline of his figure or feeling his presence nearby. A couple of years following this I remember giving a message in church and I could see this an affluent lady perhaps in her 60's whom I became aware that during her earthly life lived in a beautiful large house (possibly in Ireland). I remember giving this as a message to the circle and no one accepting, at which point the circle leader simply thanked me and suggested that maybe the lady related to me in some way. I suspect that the circle leader knew this lady was a guide rather than a spirit wanting to communicate to a loved one. Like the aforementioned monk I rarely see Emily, only catching a brief glimpse of her and a beautiful necklace she often wears.

It is interesting why I do not see Monk or Emily and it puzzled me for a long time afterwards why I would not see them when I meditated. I now look at it slightly differently and like to think they have no reason to continually prove their existence to me, it is more important that I make the effort to communicate with them through thought and feelings, rather than anything else. Over the years they've helped develop me and whilst the link I've built with them is strong I do not receive direct teachings, rather they give me subtle teachings and slow guidance over time. When I am asked to reflect or learn something, usually I am shown a vision or given a simple phrase which is profound in its meaning, I then have to learn to understand and find my own meaning. I do have two lessons from my guides that have stayed with me and are equally as profound, yet simplistic in their nature:- Whilst meditating once I was given the following phrase:

'Religion is a beautiful concept, until human emotions/ perspectives are place within it.'

I still find this incredibly profound and true for most aspects of religion, even spiritualism is impacted on by peoples own emotions or views and opinions. This is probably the only time, I have been given a statement direct from my guides; usually they show me pictures and images which I then interpret.

The second teaching goes as follows: I remember it being spring/summer time and admiring my pond prior to meditating. Upon getting rested and deep in meditation my thoughts where drawn to that pond and suddenly I became aware of how that pond reflects my life, beliefs and understanding of the world. At that moment I realised that my life was very much like a fish in a pond, in that everything I know, believe and understand are within that pond however just beyond that artificial barrier in which I live there is so much more, which I could not possibly begin to comprehend.

I feel both are pretty cool ideas and concepts, yet truly simplistic in their nature and meaning. I do hear of other mediums that claim their guides give them 'profound messages' and meanings to use in their day to day life, but I am yet to be convinced. Some of the best philosophies I have heard have come from simple thoughts or actions which are then reflected on by the medium with the aid of his/her guide. Again, I ask you to think about what point there is of a guide giving someone the answer to the meaning of life, or some other complex understanding of the universe, when they cannot prove or use it to further their spiritual development! Furthermore, who is to say that the guide has those answers in the first place? Again, I believe a lot of people hold this view, including myself when I first started out, that guides are these all seeing and knowing beings. Having done research and witnessed what I believe a handful of genuine trance experiences, I can honestly say that guides do not have all the answer, nor have any desire to be all knowing beings. I would be doubtful of any medium that makes claims such as this about their guides!

A guide can have a number of different roles when supporting the medium which includes protection, guidance and reassurance. They can also aid the process of spiritual development giving messages, healing and philosophy. Relative to the individuals point of view, will depend on how many guides they have and what their purpose is. This is particularly relevant in some kabbalah teachings whereby there are many different levels of consciousness and different guides, guiding and teaching you in different areas. Alternatively some people feel a need to have a guide for protection, and then have a guide for messages, a guide for healing, etc. Personally I am open-minded to the concept of many guides, however I would prefer to reflect on that point and understand why I need so many. Personally at the present time, Monk and Emily have stayed with me and shown me guidance and support and as far as I am aware they are the only two I work with. I am not sure if they will continue to support me or eventually move on, I will just have to wait and see. I am not one hundred per cent sure what the path holds for my guides, however I think monk is my main guide and will probably be with me throughout my life, whilst Emily may go once I have learnt the lesson I need to learn.

It is important to recognise what your guide is helping you to achieve, for me Monk is my main guide and acts as protective, almost a gatekeeping role, whilst also helping me to understand the teachings of spirit. Emily supports with helping me communicate with spirits during readings and demonstrations. Gordon Smith speaks about identifying how your guide is communicating with you through a calling card, whereby you get a signature feeling when your guide is present. This may be a feeling, or alternatively you may glimpse them and instantly know they are present. This will take time to develop and can be done through meditation and hopefully, as you get to a point whereby you can clear your mind and allow a spirit to step near, then you will feel that 'calling card'. Your teacher may take you on a guided meditation, if appropriate to help you link with your guide, this is fine and hopefully will help confirm earlier feelings.

You've probably guessed what is coming now right? You will come across 'medium/psychics' on a regular basis who say they see their guide/s clearly each time they meditate or that they are in constant contact with them. Whilst some may be able to do this, the vast majority I doubt are able to and the quality of their messages would be the evidence of this. If someone was in such direct contact then I would expect the contents of their messages to be extremely accurate. Again this is usually the people who are self-proclaimed or lack the understanding of what mediumship is actually about.

Test your guide!

I think it important to confirm your guides are real and perhaps at some point, if you feel necessary, test them and ask them to offer some proof of who they are. If you have a guide from the 19th Century for example, can they give you the place where they lived so you can check the records? Alternatively, can they give you some information which relates to them which you could study and check out. Providing you are not popping a test quiz to them every week, I am sure your guides will be more than happy to offer some information about their existence.

I have to admit, this is something I have not done and whilst writing this chapter it got me thinking about how I could test my guides and then it clicked. Emily has shown me where she lived, and it remains vivid in my mind's eye, perhaps I should do some research about properties in the Ireland area!

Protection

I want to touch on a topic now regarding protection and closing down to spirit, and how important this is, to help ensure you remained balanced. Whilst many areas of mediumship are similar, I would say this is an area where there is much difference and many varied ways to on how to balance your spiritual work and personal life. There are a number of reasons you need to learn techniques for protecting yourself, however fundamentally it is important that it works for you and you feel safe! I genuinely have conflicted views regarding the need for protection for a simple reason: I'm not convinced that there are so called bad spirits waiting to drain your energy, throw things around your house or at worst possess you! My reasons for this relates to the lack of evidence supporting such things. I think fear clouds people's judgements and what may at times be a natural occurring event or a misinterpretation of a natural spiritual event often may lead to the imagination going wild!

I have spent time in people's homes whereby a supposed evil spirit haunts the family, and have visited supposedly haunted old properties where terrible things have happened, and I genuinely believe that nine times out of ten it is the psychology of the situation, rather than some evil presence. I do not just remember one time, more a number of times when I have spoken to people about what is happening or isn't happening in their home and they are only interested in what they want to believe, rather than solving the problem. An example of this would be where you visit someone's house and discuss with them their experience, explaining that it is likely a natural occurring phenomenon, alternatively a loved one visiting the house. As part of this process I may ask my guides to protect the house in love and light and do a visualisation in mind of a white glowing bubble of energy surrounding the house. I then explain to them that it is not an evil presence rather one of the aforementioned points.

I find it interesting after visiting a number of houses often you will hear this approach hasn't resolved the problem and the person continues to experiences 'issues' and when you revisit they are unable to provide evidence of on-going phenomenon. Do not be disheartened if you are asked to visit someone's house and after you leave they continue to experience problems. Rather think about the person having the 'so-called experiences' and their own psychology. Could it be that they are needing attention, is it that they enjoy getting attention from family and friends from the belief that their home is haunted, or are they just genuinely confused!

Please do not get me wrong, I do think at times people witness phenomenon occurring at home, or when at work or public buildings, I just question the source and its supposed intentions when described as evil. I spoke to a lady recently and it became quickly apparent that she was naturally sensitive to spirits and had experienced strange phenomena on occasions. She contacted me following an experience she had when staying in an old building; describing how she awoke in the night and saw a spirit personality approach her which 'freaked her out'. As she was describing this to me, I thought that poor spirit person has probably been aware of this lady's ability to see spirit, gone up to her and got the fright of its life when the lady screamed out!

I discussed this with the lady and explained that the spirit person was probably as surprised as she was that she had become scared. It is easy to see why such an event would happen and how negative connotations could get attached to it. I explained to this lady in my opinion what had happened, and she appeared happy with that response. I have witnessed people approaching mediums and asking such questions, only to get told they were attacked by evil spirits and demons, when in fact it is not!

Having said this, I am aware of poltergeist cases which are supposed to evidence negative spirit interaction, however if true these are few and far between and with the right intervention should be managed appropriately. Often these cases are not simply a negative energy causing havoc; rather there are a number of contributing factors including the energy of the people involved, trickery/fakery and environmental factors. More research from a scientific and mediumistic perspective is required to identify the cause of such cases. For anyone interested in recorded poltergeist cases, both the Enfield case and Cardiff Poltergeist case are worth exploring. The Enfield case is a classic example of a multitude of factors possibly contributing towards the case, whilst the Cardiff Case demonstrates a different type of phenomenon and more focussed spirit activity which incidentally was not negative in nature at all. Due to popular culture and a handful of cases the word poltergeist has become associated with negative and demonic a force which is not always true.

It is interesting to note that in many poltergeist cases there is often a single person that the phenomenon is focussed around and often associated with young females experiencing the early stages of puberty. This would suggest that there is a requirement for a human agent to be involved for some phenomenon to happen, whilst also suggesting there may be unexplained psychokinetic elements to the phenomenon too. Again, when researching poltergeist phenomenon be aware that it is likely to be the most prolific cases you will come across and to think critically when reading information relating to such situations. I touch on the topic of poltergeist activity including the Cardiff and Enfield cases in more detail later on in the book.

Anyway back to protection, what is the purpose of it? Nowadays I use it as a way of helping to link with spirit, and to help recognise when I want to continue with my day to day life. Arguably it is noteworthy to reflect that if you trust your guides, why the need to ask for protection? I trust my guides explicitly, however still ask for protection as a matter of respect to them and for the job they do. There are a number of different ways you can ask and it is important to find what works for you as an individual. Asking for protection does not require silly rituals or dances to the Gods and Deities; again it should be a natural and simplistic process. The following are different ways I have seen protection being asked for which you might find helpful:

1)   Asking the Archangel Michael- This seems to be a popular one with some mediums and psychics. I do not know much of the origins with this aspect of protection; however remember if it works well for you, than use it. Perhaps you could explore with your teacher the reason why this approach is used and see if it works for you.

2)   Visualisations- initially I was taught to open my chakras and ask your guides to step forward and imagine a bubble of white/blue light cascading over to protect me whilst working. I use to do this on a regular basis and it worked well for me during my initial stages of

development. Looking back now I realise it was more a psychological need for me to safeguard myself against what was not understood.

3) Pray and asking- Since attending a further development course with Ian Nixon, I have had the opportunity to learn more about the wider processes associated with attending church services and doing public demonstrations. As part of this, I have learnt the underlying mechanics of the whole process of praying right through to closing down a circle or a public rostrum demonstration. I have chosen to adopt this into how I now open and close to spirit, and I will focus my mind (through breathing/basic meditation) and then open my chakras. At this point I will feel my guides step forward and I will ask them for light, love and protection/guidance and if appropriate say a little pray.

The third version seems to work well for me and I find it a simple quick process which then allows me to move on and work with spirit. It is definitely worth exploring different ways to protect yourself and find what makes you comfortable, I would be lying if I did not say that through my development I have not felt concerned or scared but not because of supposed spirits, rather my lack of certainty in myself and my guides. It is only over time that I have learnt to let go of my preconceived ideas about the world and started to trust. Please note over time your views are likely to change dependent upon your experiences and teachings, however use what works for you and find your own truth.

Healing:
Chapter Four

Healing
Ultimately the purpose of mediumship is to heal; heal people who are grieving and in need of reassurance. As you develop your mediumship you will find that you become more compassionate towards others including yourself. It is important to recognise the balance between compassion and taking on others grief through sympathy. At times people will want to do this either consciously or subconsciously and as a medium you need to recognise this and you need to be able to recognise how to stop it. I remember times when people have expected and at times demanded I pull rabbits out of the hat with unrealistic expectations, either because they are misguided or in deep grief. Alternatively people may see you as a guru or a go to person to give them on going guidance about their life. Remember it is important to stick to your principles as a medium or healer to ensure you have appropriate professional boundaries. It is about learning and understanding when this is taking place and you will need to be mindful of this to ensure you are not unnecessarily relied on by that person. A good teacher will help you learn techniques to manage such situations!

I remember learning this lesson a few years ago when doing a reading in church in the open circle. I remember describing the pictures a spirit person was giving me and a gentlemen stating he could understand what I was saying. Rather than accepting the information he continued to request more and more information about what I was saying and really pushing me to try and give more details. At the time I did not realise and it was only following a discussion with more established and learned mediums that they highlighted what he was doing. After that reading I felt drained and worn out, which is not what is meant to happen when giving messages, thus now when this happens I recognise the individuals conscious/subconscious attempt and don't get drawn in to such antics.

There may be times when a grieving person is desperate for confirmation and becomes frustrated at you, or alternatively expects too much from you. This is either in the message or as described above and you need to have the skills and right support to manage these situations. There are also times when someone is mentally unwell, or in deep grief and turn to you for support and help. Whilst at times this may be appropriate, you have to recognise your personal responsibility and the boundaries between your work as a medium working in private and public arenas. I remember recently where I had delivered a message to someone in church, who was clearly grieving and they asked me to help and offer emotional support to them saying that I was the only person they could turn to. It is really important to take a step back here from your ego and recognise that actually there are alternative avenues which need exploring such as local GP and other support services.

Your role as a medium is to deliver messages, remember you're not a qualified psychologist or councillor and you could make the situation far worse. I tried to be honest with this person and explained that yes, I was happy to undertake a further reading, however I could not resolve the issues going on in her life and that maybe alternative options should be explored. I think the majority of people would respect this stand point but it also allows you to show compassion whilst maintaining your personal responsibility. Remember this book is about utilising tools to help you develop as a medium, and whilst this may not a spiritual tool, it is a fundamental tool which will enable you to safeguard your role as a fledging medium.

Although healing is used during readings and messages for grieving individuals, healing itself is a practice which involves the healer asking spirit to guide spiritual energy through them, to the individual and help alleviate a physical or mental ailment. There are many different techniques, including the following:-

1) Hands on healing – whereby an individual may sit in a chair, on a bed and receive healing from a healer who uses their hands to

heal parts of the body. Some healers prefer to place their hands on the individual whereby others opt to hover their hands a couple of inches above the body and challenge healing energy from spirit.

2) Absent/Distance Healing – This is a type of healer whereby the healer or a group of healers go into a state of relaxation and ask spirit to dedicate healing to others. This can be done on an individual basis or to a wider group. I remember a medium telling me he was sat with his development group on Boxing Day 2004, when all of a sudden all their guides stepped back and left the group. It was at this point that the tsunami hit off the coast of Indonesia and their guides had gone to focus on the situation. Often when individual healers or healing groups hear of such tragic events they will spend time directing spiritual energy and spiritual thoughts to try and help those in need. I regular use this when I hear of tragic events and direct my thoughts to those in need. Alternatively as previously mentioned when I finish a meditation or reading I will ask that spiritual energy is sent to those in need. I have a lovely chocolate Labrador called Lola, who at the time of writing is eleven years old. Sadly from an early age Lola has had really bad problems with arthritis and other associated ailments. From time to time I will sit and visualise Lola and direct healing energy and thoughts to her back legs and spine. Sadly I can't tell you if she notices a different and in honesty I don't see it either but I like to think it helps her!

3) Trance Healing - I will keep this brief as we touch on trance healing a little later on in this section and then again further on in the book. Trance healing is where a developed healer/medium will allow their guide to overshadow them enabling the guide to do more direct healing. Trance healing and mediumship is a deeper level of connection with your spirit guide and takes many years to develop. Trance is often used as it allows the message or energy from spirit to be clearer, without the mediums own views and thoughts to influence the process.

Healing should be the focal point of any reading and often, my readings work so much better when a person requires healing. Let's be clear though, healing is undertaken by the message delivered rather than direct healing practices. I find this so pertinent when reading, seeing the persons face change when they realise their loved one has demonstrated their continued existence and that they are safe and watching over them. It's important to try and balance evidence from spirit against the message they are trying to deliver to ensure that the sitter gets a balanced and informative reading.

I have never had 'in-depth' healing training and if I am totally honest it's not something I want to further explore at this time. This is not because I am not interested in it, but more about my personal circumstances and commitments in everyday life. Having said that, I regularly say prays, or dedicate energy from a meditation/spiritual contact to others in need.

Becoming spiritually aware will have an impact on how you view not only your life, but also events going on around the world. It is interesting how taking time to meditate and become more aware that you begin to look at your life, the life of others in very a different manner. This was something I experienced recently when listening to the radio as I heard of another terrorist attack taking place using a car bomb. Rather than just having a binary thought process of feeling sorry for the victims and distain towards the attacker, I felt generally compassion for both. It startled me and made me sit back surprised that I felt compassion for a suicide bomber, however I realised that I was developing a deeper compassion and a deeper spiritual understanding. Rather than becoming worried about this, I simply acknowledge this thought and carried on. For me that's what healing is about, it's becoming more aware, directing positivity towards negative situations and not allowing personal feelings to cloud your judgement. In essence as a medium this is virtually the same when delivering messages, the intention is to provide clarity and accurate information which is delivered which is not clouded by your own views.

Over the years I have had the opportunity to experience healing done in different ways and it has become common place to see different types of healing advertised including reiki or crystal healing and sometimes at a considerable cost. You've probably guessed that I am critical of some of the purported healing which takes place and this is due to a number of reasons which are similar to my reasons for mediumship. True healing is a process which takes years to be develop and most of the courses available now can be done in a couple of days or at weekends which is really not appropriate. For example it is so easy to get a reiki master certificate in no time at all! I ask you to think about how effective this healing is likely to be for a supposed patient and if effective, why not adopted more widely by public services and the NHS?

Don't get me wrong, I genuinely think healing can be beneficial I know some genuine, kind healers who silently do their work with limited recognition. These are the real healers, those that sit in circles and offer healing to the wider world or undertake it in churches and people's homes. For me healing should be a natural process, which is fluid and gentle asking your guides/higher self to help bring energy to help heal the person, rather than some third level high reiki master course completed over the internet. Again it is important to ask the question for whose benefit is the show put on by the supposed healer, what benefit does it bring to their healing ability if they've accomplished a 'level three master rating?' Personally, I would rather receive healing from a novice, who has not picked up any bad habits, whose mind is clear and sincere in their attempt to help.

I recently attended a trance workshop and was blessed enough to receive healing from a lady who felt compelled to attend the event, having not had a day's training in mediumship or healing ever! I can honestly say it was the best healing I had, because she had no preconceived ideas and was genuine in her approach. It probably helped that she was being guided by one of the most genuine well known mediums around. During this event I remember seeing a lady give trance healing and was pulling ridiculous faces, wiggling her body and hands and breathing silly. I ask you this question again, why would your guides do this and whose benefit is that for? More so, what does this do to the public opinion of mediumship and healing? Luckily the medium holding the event simply advised the women to reflect on her approach to mediumship and healing. This is evident nowadays, with the general public view of a psychic being dressed up in a headscarf and looking into crystal ball, to some of the more eccentric individuals who have recently graced our TV screens.

The healing practices which I have been taught, have been about clearing your mind and asking spirit to step in and help by drawing energy to a patients area of need, whether that be an emotional problem in the aura or towards a physical problem. And remember, although healing is beneficial, this should not be overridden by a medical practitioner advice, if you've got genuine health problems, healing should accompany this and not be done in place of medical help. With regard to healing I understand that when in a calm, relaxed state the body is able to self-heal better, thus at the very least, being in an environment such as a church which is calm and relaxed is likely to have a positive impact on your emotional and physical well-being.

It's probably a good place to talk about hypnosis in this section as at times it is associated with aspects of mediumship and spiritualism, via past life regressions etc. My knowledge is very limited with regard to hypnosis, however I do know people who have benefitted from it and have seen significant changes whether that be weight loss, smoking or general anxiety. That's pretty much my limited knowledge on it, however the principles above apply. Remember not to spend ridiculous amounts of money on it, go to a trained and trusted practitioner and do not use it instead of medical advice.

I thought it would be good to interview an experienced healer, with over twenty years experiences and ascertain his views on healing, how its changed over the years and current practices. Ian Nixon, originally from Yorkshire now residing in Cleethorpes has a wealth of knowledge on mediumship and healing and I was fortunate enough to spend just under a year sitting with him in development, helping me to understand the mechanics of mediumship.

Can you tell me how long you've been a healer for?

I joined the national federation of healers in 1994 but I was an SNU healer two to three years before this. When I first started it wasn't called the SNU it was called the Guild of spiritual healers, it was under the SNU banner and that is where I did my training. When I did the exam, it was a postal style exam where you got sent a section to complete and then sent it back to get marked by the tutor, and in total there were about eight or nine sections to it. You had to get an 80 per cent pass rate and then you could apply to become an accredited healer, which I achieved. At this time, the guild was dissolving and normally I would've gone somewhere in the Yorkshire for the exam, but the only place they could fit me in was Blackpool so I went there to sit my final exam. The Exam consisted of being led into a room with four chairs and four patients and the examiner told me to start healing. The first thing I did was ask the examiners for four glasses of water, explaining that this help make the patients feel comfortable. They use to let you take charge so they could assess how you behave and how you interact whilst undertaking healing. Following this I advised the examiners that I wanted to separate the four chairs in order to make the other patients waiting feel more comfortable, sitting off to one side, whilst also allowing me to heal one person at once. After I had given healing to the patients they were given a questionnaire on their experiences of being healed. These questionnaires included questions like how did they feel, what the energy was like, what they felt my behaviour was like and how my interaction was. After this I was asked to wait whilst the questionnaires were read and then I was invited in front of a small panel who asked me questions about healing, the law and a little bit about basic anatomy. After this they turned to each other and then me and said 'I'm pleased to announce you've passed the exam and you are now an accredited healer.'

One of the things I get frustrated with, is this idea that you can attend a short course, such as a weekend seminar (reiki, alternative healing) and then get qualifications to become a 'healer'. This is just a personal opinion, but I wondered what your thoughts are on this?

Years ago the medical profession, before working with a patient a doctor had to do at least seven years before they could practice. Were in the framework I did you could do two years before qualifying to work with a patient, but the way that the SNU use to do it, you had to sit in a healing group. This was for at least three months or more, dependent upon the church you attended, before you were allowed to join. Then when you joined you could be a trainee healer for two years, during that time you would sit and take your exam, but what people were doing was coming once a month, so in actually fact they hadn't done a two year period. The SNU changed this, so you had to do a full two years. What people would do, they would join to become a healer, when in fact some people just wanted the title of a healer, so they'd turn up half a dozen times and then could take the exam to become a healer. But the idea of sitting for two years was to encourage people to get use to the energy; you'd have opportunity to learn from the accredited healers and understand how they worked and also be mentored appropriately and to safeguard the patients attending. By changing the course to a period of one hundred and four weeks, it showed the trainee healers dedication, thus removing people just seeking the title of being a healer.

With regards to different styles of healing, I don't fully understand them all but my opinion, and it is just my opinion is that it can cost a lot of money. It could be anything up to a thousand pounds for each course, but if you have the money, in a short space of time you could become an accredited healer. Like I say I don't fully understand it, but I know they use symbols and they use energy similar to a spiritual healer, where they believe (that energy) comes from, whether they class it coming from Earth energy or another source, I'm not sure. Personally when healing I believe the energy used comes from spirit, through us to the patient. There used to be an old saying 'from spirit, through spirit, to spirit'. It does seem a little unfair that other healing organisations such as the SNU, NFSA, the Surrey healers, they all have a two year period, whereas other healing routes you can become a healer within a short period of time. It is not just learning to link into the healing energy, you've also got to understand and relate to the people that you are working with. Because no two people are the same, for me when that person sits in front of me I make them feel the most important person in the world. With regards to Reiki, I couldn't really comment I know people that are reiki healers and I also know patient who say it has worked for them, more so than spiritual healing but it shouldn't make a difference which healer does the healing, but some healers are more compassionate and able to relate to other people. You could have two healers, both who have passed their exams, but one could have really good people skills as well, but it should be about the patient feeling at ease in your presents, and comfortable then they are more relaxed and not as anxious, hence they are likely to be more responsive to the healing given.

As a healer you've got to learn to adapt to the situation, to the person you're healing, a patient might not want to sit with their eyes closed throughout, or alternatively they may want to talk all the way through and you've got to learn how to deal with this and work around that. In church it is a lovely way to heal, but it is a set way and everybody knows this. When you go to a patients home, which if you do, you should always take someone with you, you should never go on your on it doesn't have to be another healer. If you go to a male/female's home, preferably you should take the opposite sex to yourself, because if there was just you and the individual there, they could accuse you of doing something inappropriate, and it can be your word against theirs. If this situation were to happen, you'd not alone bring yourself into disrepute but that of the organisation you belong to as well. They changed the rules over the years, if you were to go heal someone with a mental disorder; you were not allowed to go without another healer present. When I first going to see patients (at home) we'd usually have half an hour to an hour chatting, I'd tell them a little about myself and healing and give them opportunity to talk about themselves so you become more aquatinted with each other. At church you don't have that opportunity because as one leaves the chair, another is waiting to sit in it. I have worked in healing centres before and that is not so bad, because people would book hour appointments so if they wanted to talk or relax a little that was up to them. When visiting people at home, over the years you become friends and as soon as you're at the door the kettles on and you'd have a cup of tea for the first half an hour. I think it is all about putting people at ease, often they've heard wacky and weird stories and the idea is to help them relax.

It is fundamental that you tell people you are healing that you cannot promise anything but you cannot leave them on downer, felling negative. What I would normally say to them is that I cannot promise anything, but I have never yet had a patient who has not yet felt some benefit from healing. I have visited people have been at the end of their lives and I supported them with healing, and they have told me its help them cope with the inevitable. As a spiritual healer *from church I suppose people are sometimes interested in talking about the message side of spiritualism and the afterlife, as a national federation healer you are not allowed unless the patient brings it up, because the national federation is non-denominational and does not belong to religious spiritual body. It is a healing organisation, so you might have a staunch catholic that doesn't want a spiritualist healer round, but they might a national federation healer practice healing on them because they don't belong to anyone. The siri healers and the SNU are all connected to spiritualism so you have some connection to spirit, but a federation is non-denominational and although it is called the national federation of spiritual healers, it does not belong to a church.*

One gentleman I visited sort of believed (in the afterlife) and we talked but you never 'ram you opinions', it is important you only tell them your own experiences. I suppose this gentlemen did believe and before he passed he actually said I'm not afraid to go now, because I now I'm going somewhere now. (During this part of the interview Ian shared an experience with me about someone he gave healing on, however we both decided it was important not to break the confidentiality of the patient's story.)

When you heal people, you come across some heart breaking stories, but if you can bring comfort to somebody, than that's what is important. Personally if I go and visit someone in their own home I never charge for my services, I went to one guy and he gave five pounds and at the time I was collecting money for a blind charity and it went to them. You've heard me talk about Gordon Higginson many times, Gordon use to say is 'what we do is a vocation, not a profession.' I was very fortunate that I got most of my training through the SNU through seminars and workshops, and I was in contact with some wonderful mediums and some wonderful people and I learnt a lot from them. I also learnt a lot from spirit once I learnt to communicate with them, when your communicating with spirit it is important to recognise that that is a person to, with their own feelings and hopes. When giving messages some people deliver in a clinical way, and it shouldn't be like this. When I last worked on the rostrum as a medium somebody said I can see you love this because of the passion in your working shows. I think that's the way it should be, not think this is a job or this is something I can do to impress my friends, you do it because you love it. The pleasure of being able to help another soul, ease the mind or heart is a wonderful gift. When I deliver a development group, I say to them 'we are going to teach you to use a gift that comes from spirit but it is a gift that change people's lives and it should always change their lives for the better. It should never change it for the worse.

    A lot of people do make money out of it and that is their choice, I wouldn't say one hundred per cent that I wouldn't make some money out of it in the future but after nearly 25 years I have never made a profit from it. It is about the dedication and also the respect for spirit as well, because when you think about it, they do a lot more work than we do and if we don't respect them (spirit) than why should they respect us? I don't think it about proving you are worthy but you're dedicated about what you do. When I first started there was a guy who was in my development group with me and he said to our development leader I want to be a healer, and she said why? He responded by saying it's great to be a healer. In a nice way she tricked him and took him to one side and said 'if you real want to be a healer I can give you the number of a guy and he will make you a great healer, the only thing is the way he works no one will ever now it's you.' 'The guy turned round and said it doesn't matter!' He wanted to be known for doing it, rather than the purpose of wanting to heal others.

    I have had people ask me why I don't charge and some have suggested that money is another form of energy, you give them healing so in return they give you money as a way of thanking you, but that really doesn't sit well with me. So if somebody said to me I've got to earn a living, my response would be 'god gave you a brain and two hands, use them!' It is really important though for me to highlight, that this is just my opinion, how it works for me, I think a lot of people would agree with me, but others not. I class myself as a typical bloke and I like to work in a simple manner, because everybody can understand. If I was a clever man, which I'm not I could use high fluting words and such but there would be people like me that wouldn't understand but if I speak in simple terms then *everybody regardless of their walk of life can understand what I'm saying.*

From a spiritual perspective what are the different types of healing you are aware of?

Well obviously there is the contact healing, the laying on of hands, but just to divert a little bit, it is very rare I touch the person I usually hover my hands over the person. There is also absent healing, crystal healing, theirs sound healing. There is also psychic surgery, however there is a lot of controversy surrounding this, as you well know psychic surgeons are supposed to be able to put their hands in your body and pull things out. There is also trance healing, however the SNU didn't advocated trance healing in churches, however I recently heard that they are demonstrating trance healing at Stanstead Hall.

What qualities would you look for in a fledging healer?

To start with, I think everybody has the ability to heal to a greater or lesser degree, but it depends how much time you are willing to put into it. I would look for somebody who has a caring nature, who is a people person, somebody who has patience because you can get some colourful characters you go to heal and you have to be patience. I always say to be a healer; you've got to have a heart. I would advise anyone interested in learning more about healing to go to a local church, or go to a healing organisation, one which is a registered organisation. I would also advise them, that healing cannot be taught quickly, it takes time, most places it takes about two years to complete a healing course and it takes dedication and patience.

A final note before I move onto other topics in the book. I feel extremely lucky to have been taught the foundations of mediumship, its purpose and the mechanics by the likes of Helen and Ian. I find it sad, that individuals such as these two are almost dying breeds in the modern age of mediumship, and both have a sound understanding of what entering development should be about. Although I put my own spin and interpretation on what I have experienced over the years, ultimately the foundations of my knowledge comes from the dedicated and humble individuals I sat with in development groups.

Trance and Physical Mediumship: Chapter Five

Prior to moving onto the second part of this book, I wanted to briefly touch on two deeper levels of connecting with spirit which are less common, however if not more associated with fraudulent and ego centric 'so called mediums'. In the ten/eleven years of practicing mediumship, I can honestly say I have only seen two mediums whom I believe were entranced by spirit and two occasions whereby I have witnessed physical mediumship be demonstrated. I wanted to touch on these two subjects, because later on in the book I shall be discussing cases which touch on these subjects.

Both Trance and physical mediumship have been around for centuries, most notable during the Victoria era and World Wars when mediumship/séances and contacting the dead were either popular forms of entertainment or a way of connecting with passed loved ones in times of strife and distress, such as WW2. As with more mainstream mediumship witnessed today, both Trance mediumship and physical mediumship attract charlatans keen to make money and exploit vulnerable/gullible persons by pretending to make connect with spirit. There is a general consensus amongst modern mediums that both of these types of mediumship have declined due to the commitment required to achieve such a standard of mediumship and spiritual awareness. This partly makes sense given the commitment and time required, whereby nowadays we live in a fast paced technological world where information and answer are at the tip of our fingers and are minds are focussed on so many different things all at once. I suspect we've also seen a decline due to the public becoming more aware of science, charlatans and developing the awareness and skills to challenge things they believe not to be real.

So what is Trance? Trance mediumship at its purest involves you entering an alter state of consciousness and allowing your guide to 'overshadow you' and use your voice to communicate messages through you. There is nothing scary or mystical about this process, it should be natural and calm, with the guide communicating in a simplistic and loving manner. In its simplest form, Trance mediumship is allowing yourself to enter a deeper level of meditation and allowing spirit to communicate directly through you. The benefit of this is that it encourages purer communication from the spirit world, as when a medium communicates the information, it has more of their own interpretation of what spirit is trying to say.

As you can imagine, and in line with one of the core themes of this book I have witness my fair share of 'supposed mediums' who have gone into swaying deep trances talking in funny voices of some supposed higher being communicating about how humanity should be saved from itself! Quite frankly that is nonsense and once again the mediums imagination taking over. Whether the medium is aware of this, or sadly deluding themselves I am not sure, however any good teacher would explore this with the student and positively challenge them if they suspect it to be more about the medium rather than spirit. Again I genuinely believe it is people's lack of understanding regarding the mechanics of mediumship as the reason they misunderstand trance and go off talking in ridiculous voices and talking nonsense. No wonder the scientific community/general public ridicules the subject of mediumship if this is what the majority of people experience.

In 2015 I was fortunate to attend a day workshop led by a well-respected medium which was about trance and the using it for mediumship and healing. During the session I was struck by how simplistic and natural the process should be and the emphasis on this. During the event and whilst practising a light state of trance, the teacher commented on how my own guides were working with me. During this particularly part of the session and after coming round from the meditative set I was in, I was struck by a quite large lady stomping her feet, breathing very heavily and acting like she was in some deep trance like state. This continued as she acted as though a spirit person was channelling healing through her. At the end of the session, I was pleasantly surprised when she was challenged on this, and encouraged to reflect and ask whose purpose all that 'acting' was for. Why would spirit make you do such things? And as outlined in the book previously, whose purpose is that for? My own answer would be that it is for the person to get attention, and be seen as self-importance.

My own experiences of trance have been very limited, one of the times being the above when at a trance workshop and another experience again in 2015, when I was meditating in a group and became increasingly aware of my own heart beat and a vibrational state around my body and the sense that I might 'fly off'. During this time, I became increasingly aware of my guides drawing nearer to me and almost overshadowing. Whilst the experience was strange and different, at no point did I feel scared or concerned that I was in trouble. The experience lasted about fifteen minutes and then came to an end. What I found interesting about this experience is that another individual in the group had the same experience and described the same feelings, which is interesting as neither of us had discussed trance states that day, or had had those experiences during meditation prior. When we discussed with our teacher, he did not give us an explanation, rather just listened and encouraged us to develop our own interpretation of what took place.

Another interesting thing which I have noticed with supposed 'trance mediums', is that quite often their happy to sit and give you messages of love and light, yet are rarely able to provide evidence of survival and deliver messages. If I were to start giving trance demonstrations I would want my guides to provide evidential messages to the sitters present to confirm it definitely is spirit. Quite often you will hear trance mediums stating they are able to provide accurate information, and as result I would challenge them to do so. Not because I want you to catch them out, more to ensure that what I am listening to is genuine and truly spirit interaction. I remember sitting with a trance medium and her going into a quite convincing trance like state, in which I was able to ask questions about the spirit realms. During the session I asked the following question: *'Can you explain the nature of consciousness?'* At which point the medium appeared to be caught off guard and looked puzzled at the question before 're-entering' her state of trance to give a very basic answer to my question.

One of the very first sessions I was sat in whereby apparent trance mediumship was taking place, the lights were turned right down probably to add atmosphere more than anything, and then we waited in suspense for the spirit world to communicate, when all of a sudden the 'entranced medium' shouted 'Silence! This is Julia Caesar speaking!' Can you imagine that, a Roman Emperor visiting modern day Freeman Street, Grimsby, I wonder what he would have thought. Again I find it sad that Trance mediumship is so often associated with these fake practices, yet when demonstrated properly the messages communicated from spirit are profound and filled with love and guidance.

There is a medium locally who regular attends church and whilst his voice does change and he does sway from side to side slightly, he is to my knowledge a genuine trance medium. During his services at local churches the messages he provides are factual and accurate and offer words of encouragement and self-development.

Physical Mediumship

I do not want to discuss the topic of physical mediumship in any depth during this book, partly because it requires a book within itself, but also because it is such an abstract concept and pushes the reader's belief when not experienced directly. Again during the Victoria and War Era Physical Mediumship saw an increase in popularity with many people witnessing supposed demonstrations on a regular basis. During these periods, there were mediums who were well tested by scientists who came to the conclusion that what they witnessed was not fraudulent and was described as genuine phenomenon. On the flip side, you probably have witness séance tricks on popular magician shows such as Penn and Teller and Derren Brown, which use sleight of hand and conjuring tricks to deceive sitters that they have witnessed paranormal activity. Sadly in the Victoria era and during WW2, there were many, if not more charlatans than genuine physical mediumship.

Physical mediumship is again a type of mediumship which takes years to develop and for the reasons outlined above is in decline due to charlatans being easily caught out by a more aware general public, but also due to the time it takes to develop and the level of commitment numerous and hours per weeks and for years, before seeing any kind of phenomena happening. Physical Mediumship is a deeper altered state of consciousness which allows the spirit world to interact with energies of the medium, sitter and other energies to produce physical phenomena. When mixed together and these energies interact people witness objects levitating and spirit personalities talking/walking in and around the room. Historically this has been through the use of a substance called ectoplasm a mixture of bodily fluids which protrude from orifices of the medium and develop into materialised spirits. A good example of this would be the Harrison Home Circle which sat for years to develop this type of mediumship and a quick Google search produces some of the photos from their sessions. More common today is an alternative type of physical mediumship which uses energies from the spirit world and earth energies which enable the spirit world to produce phenomenon without the use of ectoplasm.

Unfortunately due to the nature of this mediumship, the initial stages have to be developed in the dark with the lights out and the room in complete darkness. Unfortunately this gives sceptics a good argument to articulate that phenomenon produced is done through conjuring and tricks of the sitters present. Despite this, when developed over time and properly, the phenomenon can be demonstrated in red light and in some cases full light for all parties to witness. I have been lucky enough to visit Jenny's Sanctuary in Banbury to witness a demonstration of physical mediumship, that of Bill Meadows. During the séance I witness trumpets levitating in darkness (with illuminated bands to show the instruments being used) and also a unaided harmonica being played at considerable pace darting across the room in the pitch black. All this occurred whilst the physical mediumship was strapped to a chair using cable ties and hid inside a darkened cabin. During this session and in good red light, I was able to witness a hand come out of the curtain and physically turn 360 degree which was fascinating to watch. As a reader I can understand you thinking that perhaps the medium/sitter played the harmonica or lifted the trumpets in the air, as I questioned this at the time. The main organisers involved were well into their seventies and sat at least two foot away from the cabinet which made the phenomena produced unlikely to be undertaken by them in a fraudulent manner. Also throughout the séance, random sitters where encouraged to go up to the cabinet and inspect the medium. After the séance I had the opportunity to go and inspect the room, as did others including the chair to make sure there were no tricks or illusions used. Despite my efforts I could see no trickery with the chair which would enable the medium to remove his arms and operate the harmonica or trumpet. During the séance I was able to observe the main organisation sat away from the cabinet and ensure that they were not in control of the props being used.

Gilbert Sanctuary

I thought it would be beneficial to interview someone who with a wealth of knowledge of trance mediumship and physical mediumship in order to gain an insight into what can be achieved and learnt through hard work and dedication. Here is a brief synopsis from the Gilbert Sanctuary Website:

'Gilbert Sanctuary has been founded for the Promotion of Physical Mediumship and associated phenomena. Aiming to support and aid the development of those wishing to dedicate themselves to Spirit, for physical mediumship. We have 2 private home circles, and there is No fee. Dedication Pure heart and Intent with commitment to regular attendance is necessary. Gilbert Sanctuary offers reports and audio files from séances held within it since July 2010'

Susan Filer runs the Gilbert Sanctuary in Portsmouth, United Kingdom and has over twenty five years of knowledge from home circles, physical development groups and investigating survival after death. Named after her late mother the Gilbert is a non for profit sanctuary and any profits gained are donated to Marie Curie. The following is a transcribed of an interview I did with Susan Filer regarding her work at Gilbert Sanctuary and also her knowledge of mediumship, predominantly Physical mediumship. It is perhaps worth mentioning at this point, all the people I have interviewed in throughout this book have spoken about the dedication, respect and length of time is required to work with spirit. Each person emphasises the importance of highlighting that far from spirit serving us, it is about working in partnership with them and enabling the collective consciousness to develop and build our knowledge and understanding of what awaits us once we reach the end of our earthly life.

If you could tell a little about the Gilbert Sanctuary and your role there?

The Sanctuary itself is a converted sacred space in my home and the basis is to show as many people that there is life after life. Prior to this we had mental mediumship demonstrations here and prior to that I did a lot of (spirit) rescue work in rescue circles. But the sanctuary itself is all synchronistic, spirit directs you in my opinion, experienced opinion and what I believe, I don't believe in dogmatic views, everybody's reality is different. When we pass that is when we all know a little more. On reflection I was directed by spirit to build this sanctuary to promote physical mediumship and associated phenomenon dependent upon what that is, as physical mediumship can be divided into two categories including evidence from spirit/loved ones and then phenomenon, which both are evidential and often go together.

The principle of the sanctuary was originally to have home circles and to provide a safe place for practising mediums to develop, so we have 1:1 cabinet work for trance mediums or for trance mediums that would like to try and go deeper and currently we have three groups here, were individuals are learning and developing. We also host public mediums at the sanctuary, inc. Bill Meadows, Warren Clayor, the Rainbow Circle, Sandy Thorpe and Kai Muegge when he is in the country, which sadly is not very often. Every three or four months there is always a séance here, and at the moment Elaine Thorpe is developing quite amazing levels of deep trance, the other thing which I would have here as with other demonstrations it needs to be akin to physical is psychic surgery, so sometimes Vince Fuller visits and does a demonstration.

The energy that is here is wonderful, it's all about service, humility and demonstrating survival. Sadly their appears to be issues relating to some mediums ego's, they don't realise we are a vessel (for spirit to communicate) and it is not about the individual, it is about spirit, like Stewart Alexander after 45 years, who is here in a couple of months, I have never seen such a humble man. I think it is quite amazing that someone has gone on that journey with so much adoration, for me he is the icon of how a physical medium should be. Spirituality and mediumship and they don't always go together and for some it takes a lot of time to realise that. Some people think mediums are next to god and beautiful people and I'm afraid it doesn't always work like that.

We have some lovely phenomenon here but as you know, physical mediumship takes about six to twelve years it's about sitting in service, in the love, in the energy and anything that you get is icing on the cake! You have to sit, hoping to enable spirit to communicate in a physical way. What I am finding with it (the phenomenon) that it is developing here all the time, and I am sure it is spirit led. It is also becoming a mini education centre and I think as the gilbert forum develops I get more enquires and I always say this is my opinion, this is how I work you need to find your own way but I'll tell you what I know and then you need to modify that to what your spirit team want.

Are you a practising/developing medium yourself?

No I sit for physical mediums, I don't practise from the point of view of doing platform and that's not knocking platform, thirty five years ago that how I started at the Joseph Carey Psychic foundation. I have sat in rescue circles, I have run mental mediumship groups at Gilberts Sanctaury over the years here but at the moment I sit for physical mediums that are developing.

What has working with spirit taught you about life here and survival after death?

It has taught me basically and again this is opinion we're here to learn love and compassion and that is all there is at the end of the day. That is what is has taught me, love and support is what it is all about, it is quite simple really. It is about walking your walk, helping others, love and compassion. Regarding survival after death, my views haven't changed I have always known we survive after death. I had experiences from quite an early age, but has time has gone on that has developed moving from one aspect of mediumship to another where it has reached a point where I have the opportunity to experience, materialisation, direct voice and other phenomenon, these experiences have left me with no doubt we survive bodily death. Essentially we are spirit in human form, I love the expression 'I know, I don't believe', knowing is having absolutely no doubt.

I really rate Colin Fry both his mental and physical mediumship, I really love his simplistic thoughts on mediumship, he says to be a medium you got to have a level of compassion, healing and counselling and I think that is so beautiful, but also he speaks about understanding your limitations and recognising when an individual needs referring on to a GP, or other health professionals. It is important to recognise when an individual needs help not from a medium but other types of support, and essentially having personal responsibility as a medium. As Colin Fry states mediumship can heal or it can harm and part of that role is understanding personal responsibility and recognising when something else is required. Spirituality is how you conduct yourself, how you behave, your intentions, your humility, some people involved in spiritualism think they're so highly spiritual but they always understand what that means.

<u>Can you tell me some of the phenomenon you witnessed over the year, when witnessing physical mediumship and is there anything that really stands out in your mind?</u>

I think all of it really, it is difficult to say because if you think about it direct voice and materialisation is amazing, so is levitation, apports and ectoplasm are all amazing as well so where do you draw the line? If you think about it, here at the Gilbert Sanctuary it is a small private venue we only take twelve people at sittings so what I see and experience here is quite amazing, I am six inches away from the cabinet and the mediums control, it makes all I experience amazing. The direct voice, the concept of talking directly to spirit, similar to talking with you, but all of it is amazing and I am sure will get more in the future when we get materialisation in the light. In honesty about it is sitting, it's not about philosophy or always asking questions, it's about giving your love, giving your energy with no expectations, that's when you get everything. Also what is amazing is that spirit trust you so much, to be able to sit there with spirit talking to you through direct voice, in red light with the medium ungagged providing further evidence it is not the medium talking with production of ectoplasm is wonderful.

<u>You mentioned witnessing phenomenon in light, is that something which you are currently working towards?</u>

I think this is a huge debate in physical mediumship, same as thermal imaging, even with physical mediums like Bill Meadows I find now they are using a lot more red light than previously. I would say everybody is moving towards working in the light. It is so simple, spirit are the bosses and you have to follow want they want, critics will argue that is an excuse the medium is using but spirit do articulate they understand that people need evidence but they can only do it their own time. If physical mediums start in the light, it would take ten times longer to get any phenomenon occur, but overtime the chemist, engineers in the spirit world will be able to work towards producing phenomenon in the light. We have recently been advised by some guides here during séance's for the séance room door to be opened, allowing earth energy in and sitters to get cameras and take pictures, this in itself is progress. I understand that it is slow progression but I don't mind that, it's about what spirit and what they need to do to keep the medium safe. I have seen some mediums, in candle light, oil light and red light and this is increasing, and spirit are progressing in their own time.

What people need to understand is it is about working as a team with spirit and developing together, it is also depends on what level of understanding the spirit team have as well, because there are billions of realms in the after world and we go where are vibrations are suited, but it doesn't mean once you pass you immediately know everything. This is partly why we get conflicting views about the spirit phenomenon, you might get one trance medium give an opinion on reincarnation and then another give a totally opposite view, it's purely that individual spirits level of understanding and each of them are learning over time. They told us at Gilbert Sanctuary a few years ago through a trance medium, this would always be 50/50, their learning, our learning, and it is about teaching each other. And how wonderful is that, that spirit recognise this and there's no ego involved, spirit appreciate their opportunity to come to a circle and work with us for that allotted time, as long as we are there giving our energy and allowing them to experiment as a team.

What tips would give to someone wanting to develop medium?

If I was talking to anybody about whey they wanted to get involved in medium, I would ask them what is your intent? Why are you wanting to do it? Referring back to Colin Fry says 'if you want to be famous push off and go on X Factor!' I think that is lovely, it gets the point across that mediumship is not about ego, showing off or being famous, it is about being in service and first of all you are in service to god, than in service to people and then your are in service to spirit.

If a person is asking about how to develop, I would advise them to go to a good private circle and get a good mentor so they are able to get that good advice and support. To become a medium, you need to have experienced have a bit of joy in life, a bit pain and a few grey hairs, but also recognising you cannot don't do this for six months and then be a medium demonstrating on the rosturm, it takes time, a long time with patience, love and there's no rush. Going public to soon, certainly in a physical sense is the biggest mistake people make, and I am sure this must be the same with regard to mental mediums as well. Essentially your role as a medium or healer is to serve mankind; it is about looking at yourself and your place within life and ensuring that during development you get good support. It isn't just about sitting in a group once a week, it is about taking time to sit as an individual between groups on your own and meditating enabling spirit to work with you and blend with you overtime. It takes personal dedication from the individual to develop that relationship with spirit, doing this two or three times a week, it takes great effort from spirit to work with us, so it is important to give yourself to them between circles.

For the group we have a Gilbert, it took two years for the energies to blend and for us to receive the level of phenomenon now and people *need to understand that it takes time and requires patience. If you consider the spirit in this, if you have changes in your group, particularly in a physical circle it can takes them months to get the energy right again. We have had spirit ask us before to try and prevent the changes in groups as it sets them back and I feel so sorry for spirit when this happens and the impact it has, but equally isn't it wonderful that they do that and they start again, they don't have that ego. The one thing I really look forward to at the point of passing, is understanding how difficult it is for them to communicate with us on a mental and physical level. Even for the natural mediums, it takes time to develop phenomenon, and I talk to a lot of private groups that have wonderful phenomenon.*

Burnout

In March 2015 I decided to publish a Facebook page offering readings and also giving advice about mediumship. I decided to do this after becoming frustrated at not working on the rostrum and also witnessing poor mediumship often charged at extortionate rates. During that year I did many readings often spending time throughout the week and weekends travelling around Grimsby and the North Lincolnshire giving readings in people's houses, all this whilst trying to have a marriage, raise two kiddies, have a full time job and extra post graduate training.

Fast forward to the beginning of 2016 and I began to notice changes around me, my readings became more inconsistent, with less evidence and my personal life became increasingly difficult to manage and balance. This led me to make the sad decision to close my page as overtime I realised I had become burnt out and exhausted from everything I was trying to juggle. Burnt out in mediumship and everyday life is not uncommon and most dedicated mediums are likely to experience it at some point in time. As a result my link with spirit suffered and no longer could I communicate or relay messages. In no way do I blame the spirit world from pulling back as it is my responsibility to look after myself, manage my energy/time and experience everyday life. Remember ultimately we are here to learn, experience the high, lows and in-between times during our earthly existence, which is a fundamental part of growing spiritually.

A final thought on mediumship.

As I come to the end of this first section, I have reflected on the varied and somewhat different styles of mediumship I have come to witnessed. The above is what works for me and is based on my values including critical and analytical thinking which I have developed through my work and scientific qualification. I genuinely think mediumship should be a process which is natural and based in evidence, which at the present much is not. Mediumship takes years to develop, to understand the subtle energies and the signs and ways spirit can communicate with you. It is a process whereby you need to soak in as much information and then sift through to come to your own truth. I have seen many bizarre and strange things whilst developing mediumship and unfortunately often this relates to a person's personality, rather than spirit itself.

Giving messages or healing is about providing evidence for survival after spirit, not about your ability to be clever or super spiritual. By using the above techniques the messages you deliver become more accurate and require less interpretation from you and your own life experiences and values. Sadly this is a point which many mediums do not understand and is the reason why I continually draw the reader's attention to this throughout the previous chapters.

If you are a medium or wanting a reading I urge you to always question and always be true to yourself. Do not be afraid to challenge and question peoples beliefs and assumptions in an inquisitive nature. The general public recognise the difference between those who are egoistically in their mediumship and those who are genuine. By following the steps I have outlined on the previous pages allows you to have a system which is structured, about developing spiritually and enables you to enhance the clarity of your messages.

Don't be afraid to stand out from the generic and trust in spirit, but remember to keep yourself grounded.   I am lucky to have friends which challenge my beliefs and wind me up about seeing spirit, this helps to keep me grounded and reminds me of whom I am. Don't surround yourself with only spiritual people as you will likely feed each other's egoistically beliefs and lose perspective on everyday life and its problems which ultimately are important lessons to experience.

Part Two: Wider areas associated including the paranormal field

Ghostly Experiences and a brief discussion on ghost hunting:
Chapter Six

<u>My ghost experiences</u>
I thought it would be good to discuss some of the times I have witnessed ghostly phenomenon in everyday life. I must stress that when I see spirit or ghost when not focussed on delivering messages it tends to be random and happens unexpectedly. I must admit I find it a wonderful experience when I get the opportunity to see ghostly activity as it can be exhilarating but also gives further confirmation that I am actually sensing extraordinary things. I remember visiting the ruins of an old monastery abbey in North Yorkshire and catching a white robe figure walking into a building. This surprised me as I thought I would have seen a traditional monk style of clothing, if I was to see a ghostly figure at all. Upon reading the plaques in one of the side buildings, I noted that the monks who previously resided there did wear white gowns. For me its little bits of evidence which helps provide proof that what I am seeing is in fact something which I am genuinely experiencing.

It is important to draw a distinction between ghost and spirits at this point. I think the best example of distinguishing what is a ghostly phenomenon and what is spirit interaction is as follows. A ghost is where you may witness the typical brown hooded monk walking across your path; or the roman soldiers marching down the road. This are often described as a memory which are perceived by the person and almost a 'downloading of information' from the environment. A ghost will not interact with you and more importantly has a no conscious or awareness, it's like a visual memory. Another good example would be that of the ghost which is seen at the same time each year at the same point, such as perhaps a grey/green or blue lady dependent upon the area of the country you live! Often people witness these events and become scared and frighten and I can appreciate why, given how bizarre such an experience can be. I like to think, it's almost a psychic experience which the person is tuning into, and they've subconsciously downloaded that information and become aware of it.

Spirit interaction is different, in that theirs a consciousness and awareness in a spirit person. Often people who experience a spirit encounter it will be of a loved one, or a person trying to get a message across. A good example of this would be the smell of the deceased favourite perfume, when no one else is in the room, or the feeling that someone is watching over you, or on more rare occasions, whereby the spirit person is seen and communicates with the living. There are many different types of spiritual encounters some which will be touched on later in the book. These experiences are not there to frighten you; they are about giving you reassurance and evidence of the continuation of the human consciousness.

The stories that I have shared below are a collection of the most memorable experiences which I have had. At the time, some were frightening not because that was the intention, but because of my lack of understanding. Nowadays when things like this happen, I often smile and think how lucky I am that I've witness such events.

1) Hewdens Ghost

This is probably the first true experience I had of spirit interaction. At the time it frightened the life out of me and for months after I refused to enter that workshop on my own. After leaving school I took on an apprentice-ship as a plant mechanic at a local chemical factory. I recall being told stories of ghostly figures which would walk around the site, previous workers who had spent time on the site throughout their earthly life. There were reports from a gentleman I worked with (Fred) that there was a ghostly presence in the workshop, and I must admit looking back it did have an atmosphere about the place. In fact the same man I worked with spoke of times where he had heard people pottering about the workshop at night and how he would often call to the supposed spirit 'put the kettle on!'

During those days, I vividly remember willing myself to see a ghost or have a ghostly experience for confirmation. The workshop itself was a large hanger type building which was situated away from other contractors and in its own compound. Inside the workshop it was open planned with a clear view to the back of the building where there was a large metal cage from one side of the workshop to the other, with the back of the workshop in clear view. To the back right of the workshop there was a radio plugged in and next to the radio and in front of the large cage there was a set of steps leading up to a small upstairs area above the cage; again which was open planned so anyone up there could be viewed.

I remember walking up to the radio to change it to a national radio station more suited to my taste and as I approached I heard large heavy footsteps running up the stairs. Remember at this point I had no previous experiences of ghost/spirit interaction and as you can imagine it frightened the life out of me, with me immediately running out of there and for months after refusing to go in without someone else present. I do not recall telling others about that experience, probably because I would have been ridiculed but I found it a mind blowing experiences. To this day I genuinely believe that was my first real ghostly experience, given that no one could have ran up those stairs and hid without me seeing. Further to this, the steps were so clear and so loud it was not anything from the site or anywhere else in the compound.

If I am honest, I am not sure why I experienced that, perhaps the months of wishful thinking and waiting for an experience I finally got what I asked for, either way at the time it had a profound effect on me. If that were to happen nowadays, I'd probably react in a calmer and less fearful manner. I also like to think that I would recognise such an experience was about to happen and appreciate it more. To categorise the experience I would say it was more a spirit interaction, rather than ghostly experience, but who and why, to this day I still don't know......

2) A local suicide spot

It is such a tragedy when someone feels the need to take their own life, when they no longer feel as though they can cope with their problems. It is really important for me to highlight at this point, that when someone takes their own life or die in horrendous circumstances that once on the other side they do not suffer. More importantly they are not judged, punished for their actions, they are given healing and time to reflect on their actions. I find it absolutely repulsive to think that this view is still shared with grieving relatives.

Unfortunately near where I live in Lincolnshire, there is a local spot where over the years many people have decided to end their life. I remember walking my dogs down the local embankment and witnessing police and rescue services dealing with someone who had recently taken their live and I would not be surprised if it is a common sight for regular walkers/bikers in that area.

I have two boisterous chocolate labs that require regular long walks, one of which is situated near this local suicide spot. I remember walking up the embankment with my dogs and looking down the road and thinking I saw a man stood next to an old gate. Assuming it was the trick of light I carried on sorting out my headphones when again I looked up and saw the brief shadowy figure I had seen previously. Within a flash it had disappeared and I continued with my walk pondering what I had seen. Upon coming up to the gate I notice flowers and ribbons attached to it which were fresh and obviously been placed within the last day or so. As I approached I read one of the cards which had the name of a man on and words of sorrow from a friend. For me this was confirmation of what I had seen and instantly I sent compassion and healing thoughts to the individual and his family/friends. At the time, I think the gentlemen showed himself to demonstrate that he was safe and in no way in harm. I got no sense of fear from this person or that he wanted help, more that he wanted to show someone he was safe. At the time I thought at some point I may have ended up reading for one of his family, but this has yet come to fruition. Again I would class this as a spiritual encounter rather than the ghostly presence of someone who unfortunately took their own life.

I feel it is important for me to mention at this point, that I had no expectations when walking down there to see a ghost/spirit and to my knowledge had not heard the news of a local death. I mention this, because some would argue that I was subconsciously expecting to see something, when in fact I was more focussed on getting the right songs sorted for my dog walk.

3) Kettle/phone

This is an incident which took place in my home and to be honest I do not think it was a ghost or a spirit, rather a change in energy in and around the home. Both these incidents happened separately but both with my then wife present. The first occurred when we were stood in the kitchen talking and then heard a click to our right and saw the kettle turn on! It could be argued that it was surge in the energy or a fault with the kettle both which rightly so, are appropriate points of view to articulate. However it is also relevant to question if there was a change in energy which caused the kettle to turn on. Again I must emphasise, I do not have evidence to support such a 'theory' and I use the term as a general phrase, however if spirit are communicating with us and manipulating the surrounding areas, then this could arguably happen.

The next experience took place separately to the above incident, but equally strange. This again happened in my kitchen (common theme) and I had my phone on a shelf approximately 6ft high and it moved off the shelf and landed a few metres away on the floor. Now due to where I had positioned it on the shelf it could not have fallen and also given its trajectory it falling off in a horizontal direction becomes less likely. I am not in any mean's suggesting that a spirit threw my phone or turned on the kettle, more that energy around us can be influenced either by changes in the environment or perhaps faulty electrics.

I recently had a family member tell me there new home was haunted due to a glass 'flying' of the side and smashing on the floor and also the hoover turning itself off. I tried to explain my opinion that perhaps the energy within the new home and the mixing of the new exciting energy of the family created an 'energy burst' which made the glass move, or indeed the hoover turn itself off. Interestedly she looked bemused at my suggestion, opting to believe that it was a ghost instead!

Many people make assumptions that naturally occurring events are immediately spiritual or paranormal in nature. Essentially this is a type of 'confirmation bias' where believers and sceptics alike formulate an opinion of information that suits their own personal views rather than taking a critical and reflective perspective. It is really important when studying spirituality and/or the paranormal that you keep an open mind, and challenge people's views and opinions in a realistic and critical manner. It is noteworthy at this point to highlight that theories cannot be made up without some supporting evidence. A good example of this is the idea quantum healing, which purports to use quantum energy's to heal patients, despite a serious lacking in a solid evidence base. Remember always ask where's the evidence, the proof? Often scientist and sceptics will use examples such as the above to disprove mediumship/psychics/healers because people try to develop a view which is ill informed and based on confirmation bias.

On the subject of quantum physics, I must stress that there are elements of quantum physics which are spooky in nature and react in bizarre and unique ways, but that does not automatically mean it explains or should be associated with the paranormal. Whilst I personally believe that quantum mechanics may play a role in how spirit interact with us; I am cautious before spouting such an opinion as factually. I would want some peer reviewed evidence to support this and until that day, it remains an opinion/view rather than actual fact.

4) The ghostly phone call

If I had to discuss two poignant moments in my spiritual development with regard to ghostly/spiritual experiences, the Hewden's ghost and this next experience would be the two I would pick. I appreciate what I am about to discuss may appear abstract and sound bizarre, but I am genuine when stating that this did happen and not only did it have a profound impact on myself as a developing student but also the teachers I worked with at that time. Since that time I have not experienced anything like this; however having spoken to other people it would appear that it happens more than I previously thought.

This certain experience happened in the early days of my development and on reflection I realised how limited my knowledge was on many facets of the paranormal and spirituality during this time. My early development consisted on three important areas: a) meditation, b) spiritual awareness c) tools to communicate. I was lucky enough to receive 1:1 tuition from an established medium and her partner who had a good understanding of energy, and how to utilise it when working with developing mediums. Initially much of the work focussed on meditation, understanding basic energy's and developing awareness of spirit. As this progressed I was shown different techniques for contacting the spirit world and on one of these evening we tried a technique called scrying.

Scrying is a technique where a tool such as a crystal ball, mirror or reflective object is used to see and communicate with spirit people. During this evening we had a number of different experiments being undertaken including using a candle, a mirror and water. Each evening we always made sure that we offered a pray and asked for guidance and protection, with this evening being no difference. The evening started the same as any other and different experiments wielded different results, responses and discussions about the pros and cons of using these tools, but then things started to change. The energy in the room became more and more intense, with both Helen (teacher) and Tony starting to experience more intense visions and feelings when scrying. Helen began to describe quite clear visions she was experiencing whilst Tony was describing a vision of a man and the name George being said over and over in his mind and some connection to the Black Death. As a result of the increased activity we decided to stop the experiments and draw the evening to a close and allow for time to discuss and reflect on the evening's events.

Upon closing ourselves and the experiments down and all feeling a little uncertain about what we had experienced, Tony plugged the telephone back in and as he walked away it began to ring. Upon answering the phone, Tony sounded and looked surprised and from what I could initially interpret Tony was trying to reassure the gentlemen on the other end of the phone. Upon Tony putting the phone down, it then rang again and this time Tony became adamant and starting stating, 'I'm sorry, but no we have not called you!' This carried on for a short time, with Tony eventually unplugging the phone and then told us that the gentlemen in question was called George and wanted to know why we had been ringing him all evening! Tony is a big built gentleman and not frightened easily but I think it's safe to say that both of us were quite perplexed and in all honesty a little startled. Towards the end of the evening it became clear that for whatever reason our experiments attracted a number of different spirit personality to the property and the room felt full to the brim with different spirit personalities. I can honestly say being in that energy, was one the strangest sensations I have ever experienced.

So why did this happen and what was its purpose? After the session, Helen liaised with her guides who promptly responded asking us to consider how we ask for protection and the tools we use to communicate with spirit. At the time, I was quite perplexed and frightened, looking back now I understand that spirit where teaching us a lesson and it was only my interpretation of the situation which made it frightening, not the experience itself. The lesson I took from that evening was about recognising when communicating with spirit that you need to understand when using such tools that you can attract different energies who may want to communicate. On reflection I no longer feel scared, more intrigued that spirit can engineer energies around them and use this to communicate with us in the physical world.

5) Spirit photography (aura)

This one is not my story but that of my previous mentor and now friend Helen Bibby. Aura's as previously discussed are the energies around a person or object and Aura photography is supposedly a process which captures the colour of an individual's aura. I say supposedly because I am not fully sure how they work and how they capture the different and vibrant colours in and around a person's aura. I have previously had my aura photo taken which consists of you placing your hands on two mental hand palms and a photo being produced by a camera which is Polaroid type. Some mediums/psychics will then use this as a way to give the sitter you a reading and interpret the different colours to give guidance and advice.

I remember hearing discussions about how spirit persons can show themselves within your aura and believe me every time I sat for one of those photos I willed my relatives, pets, old neighbours and guides to show themselves in the photo, which unfortunately never happened. Having said this I remember talking with Helen at the time and she told me a story about how her guide, White Cloud had shown himself in her aura photo laughing. Now bizarre as this may seem, when Helen asked White Cloud to explain he was laughing and told her as a native Indian when they first encountered cameras they believed they captured the soul, hence why he showed himself laughing. Unfortunately at the time, Helen could not locate the picture due recent house moves and it took a year or two later for me to finally see this picture and from what I can remember, you clearly see a face, which looks like a Native Indian and he is clearly laughing. I wish I could publish this photo, however since speaking with Helen since, it is my understanding that the picture has faded and no longer can you clearly see a face.

6) Nurses and doctors

This is an experience I had whilst on placement when in my final year of university in 2011. At the time I was working for a local authority and the offices were situated at an old hospital site. On two separate occasions, I saw separate ghostly memories in different parts of the bundling. I must admit, when on your own in the building it was at times atmospheric, which probable could be put down to the old style doors, the long cold corridors and uneven floors.

The first experience occurred when I was walking into the office corridor and noticing out the corner of my eye, a gentleman sat at a desk in a brown suit that appeared to writing or reading documents. Now at this point I had become use to these little visions, but as always it was a lovely surprise to witness a vision in the middle of my working day.

The second experience is slightly different, and offered me an opportunity to explore the vision and gain some confirmation. I remember walking up the stairs and becoming aware of a vision in my head rather than in front of me of nurses wearing old style uniforms and stood smoking in the stair well. Now this surprised me a little because I had not expected to witness this type of vision, nor for the nurses to be smoking in the building. Luckily I developed a friendship with a secretary who in her younger years had been a nurse and when I mentioned my ghostly vision to her, she was able to confirm that this use to take place in the corridors and nurses would have been working in that vicinity of the building. I find visions like this one interesting because subconsciously I would not expect to see nurses stood in a corridor smoking, which begs the question why I would imagine such a vision.

It is probably important to mention at this point, that these visions do not scare me, nor are they something I expect every person to witness, however I do feel that when you go into a building, whether old or new, you get a vibe and an extension of that vibe can lead to you picking old memories within it. How often do we hear people say that felt at home when they walked into a house they want to buy, or they get a distinct feeling they do not like a place, for me this is the psychic element of a person at work, it's a sensory part of who we are.

7) Sensing spirit at work.

This is an experience I had when in a previous job whereby I was talking to someone about a life experience and became aware of a golden spirit person stood behind them, which felt male in its energy. Soon after I saw this spirit, the person I was in discussion with told me that his brother had previously died in an accident. Now as referred to before, I am not a psychic or medium which sees spirit everywhere I go and these experiences I have written about have been over many years; but again for me this gave me confirmation that the things I sometimes sense are reality and sometimes, for whatever reason I am able to sense their presence.

It is perhaps important at this point to talk about how I see spirit people, as I often see them in different forms. As outlined above sometimes I might see a faint golden outline of a spirit person, whereas other times I will see a vision in my head, or a fleeting physical image just out the corner of my eye. At other times, I have a strange experience whereby I almost can feel a spirit person stood behind a individual but feel this with my eyes. This may sound strange but it is the only way I can describe this experience and even to me it sounds weird!

I mention the different ways I see spirit to encourage you as a developing medium to keep an open mind and be prepared to sense spirit in different ways. Whilst I do often see spirit, at times I will also feel their presence, as well as smell and feel conditions they may have had. It took me a number of years to truly understand that spirit communicate with you in so many different ways. Once I got past the notion of expecting to see spirit stood in front of me, my mediumship grew and communication became clearer.

8) Walking the dog ghost

This final experience stands out in mind, purely because of how crystal clear I saw this image. At that time, I had two boisterous Chocolate Labradors who required daily morning walks, and one of the places I walk them is a small park behind my house. I had walked down this little cutting behind some houses on many occasions and just before the end of the cutting I saw a girl about six years of age stood, in a white Victorian style dress with her head down looking at the ground. It was amazing to see her so clearly, if only for a brief for seconds, especially when my mind was far from thinking about spirit persons, or seeing ghostly figures. I am pretty sure what I saw was just a memory of yester years and I doubt I will see her again, however I wonder from time to time, if anyone else has spotted this young lady stood there.

Ghost Hunting

Ghost Hunting…….. What can I say about this! I have mixed feelings about ghost hunting and its role in contacting the spirit world. I have such mixed feelings because of the experiences I have had both positive and unfortunately negative as well. Further to this I have mixed feelings about the idea that spirits linger in places trapped for many years at a time, I don't understand the purpose of this and it is certainly not something I have experienced. Having said this, when I took active interest in paranormal investigation I did witness some extremely interesting things, which I believe could not be explained by normal means.

I wanted to write about ghost hunts and investigations to shed a light on some of the good work which goes on, but also the often poor and misguided practice that people are often subject to on events in and around the country. If you recall at the beginning of the book I mentioned my interest in most haunted and as part of my initial interests I wanted to investigate the supposed paranormal goings on in around and the country. As a result I was fortunate enough to spend time in different locations in the Lincolnshire and surrounding area investigating many different venues, including old halls, military sights and the occasional pub.

I quickly became frustrated with a number of things which challenged my thinking, the first being the supposed scientific minded members of each team and the 'techniques' used to capture paranormal phenomenon. Often there would be a presumption, a starting point that activity captured is ghost related, when in fact the starting point should be an independent stand taking account of the wider factors first and the last resort being paranormal, secondly the lapse and varied styles of collecting information. Their seemed to be no protocol for collating relevant and accurate data, which could then be examined and compared; in fact often there was an over reliance on gadgets not designed for 'hunting ghost' such as EMF meters, inaccurate use of voice and video recording devices. It is also an interesting question to ask as to why groups feel the need to investigate in the dark, when in fact, most ghost/spirit sightings are in the daytime. Often reasons were given to me, that it is easier for spirits to communicate, however I would argue that most people do it for the atmosphere and related thrills wandering around a darkened building during the evenings and getting scared.

I have recently come across a blogger called Hayley is a Ghost Geek, and whilst there are elements of her blogs I do not share the same views on, often Hayley is right with regard to the poor practice so often portrayed by many different groups. Further to this, I am aware of a group called Para.science, which use strict scientific controls and procedures for collating and analysing data collected during an investigation. Para.science also publishes elements of their work for public scrutiny, which many groups often do not.

The reason for discussing the above, is to highlight again the theme running through this book and to ensure that people have an awareness between what is true scientific research and what is pseudoscience masked as the real thing. Groups throughout the land will use gadgets, the darkness, a supposed psychic and other psychological techniques to trick people or to unknowingly deceive themselves into thinking they are communicating with the spirit world. A good example of this is, is the use of an electromagnetic field detector (EMF Reader), used by groups to apparently detect nearby spirits, a device which in everyday life should be used by electricians, rather than ghost groups. Often this device is swung about and when the lights trigger on the device indicate this is a sure sign you are communicating with the unseen world, when in fact it proves nothing at all. This device is not scientifically tested to be used when communicating with spirits, if so I am sure more electricians would be perplexed by the strange electrical readings they pick up when installing equipment.

Remember, any group which purports to offer scientific ghost investigations to the public are in actual fact offering an entertainment company. Whilst they may state their techniques are scientific, these are likely to be very lapse in nature due to the type of environments these events take place. I also wonder how many of these groups, are actual 'scientist' rather than self-proclaimed, whilst having an academic qualification is not always necessary, it helps to develop critical and analytical thinking which arguably is fundamental in any field of science.

Don't get me wrong, these events can be fun and for people interested in the paranormal and enjoy feeling scared or frightened then these events are worth going on, just be aware that there for entertainment only and are not true scientific investigation of the paranormal. One final thought on ghost hunting remember if you catch an orb, it most definitely dust and not a ghost.

Demons and the occult!

I recently sat in an open circle and watched a 'medium' stand up and begin to tell a women (in a silly voice) in front of thirty or more people, that this person had a 'dark, dark energy' in their house. Well, if you've read the previous chapters I am sure you can imagine the sheer horror on my face at this women's statement. During the circle I had to stopped the women and ask her to deal with it at the end. After the circle I approached the 'medium' and gave an explanation as to why I had to interrupt and it was apparent that she was somewhat annoyed stating: 'I give things directly from spirit and from my guides!' I am one hundred per cent convinced that spirit would not ask a medium in a room full of people to tell the recipient they have dark or nasty energies in their home. Safe to say, I have nothing to do with this said medium and her poor mediumship practise.

Ouija Boards and other tools for communicating with the other side

There is much controversy surrounding the use of Ouija Boards and much conflict in whether or not they should be used as a tool to communicate with those on the other side. I recall walking past the old church where I grew up in my early teens and being fascinated and scared when seeing an Ouija leant up against the church wall, instantly with thoughts about demons and the occult.

Ouija boards are discouraged by many stating that they enable supposed evil entities or mischievous spirits to manipulate the persons using the board. I personally have never experienced anything negative when using an Ouija board and when deciding to use them I have always done it in a controlled environment and offering appropriate protection. I think people that do experience problems with them results from lack of understanding, fear and also not using protection. An element of people's misunderstanding most likely comes from the group response and this escalating into hysteria.

My advice if using a Ouija Board, is to ensure that you are with people you trust and who have an understanding in how to use them, including asking for protection and guidance from a higher force. From a purely sceptical perspective it is interesting to note that in some countries the Ouija Board in its original format is a board game aimed at young teenagers.

Table Tipping

Table tipping is a communication tool dating back to the Victoria Era when Spiritualism was at its early heights. Table tipping consists of individual's sat around a table usually with the guidance of a medium and then ask spirit to knock, move or lift the table. During the years I have studied mediumship I have never seen a table lift off the ground and whilst I have seen pictures and videos purporting to demonstrate this, usually these are not done in controlled environment. Sometimes the phenomenon is achieved by placing a glass upside and each individual lightly placing a finger on, then encouraging spirit individuals to move the glass around the table and in response to questions asked.

It could be argued that when the table or glass is moved this is either someone faking by influencing said item or alternatively by the participants unknowingly moving them unconsciously. I would say in most cases both of these answers are correct and both probably play a part in most attempts when individuals partake when out on public investigations. I have attempted to get a response when doing both of these techniques and on more than one occasion I have been suspicious that sitters have been subconsciously pushing or moving them along, however there have been times when this has not been the case. Usually when using a glass and it begins to move and we get answers to questions I pick a random participant and ask them to remove their hand and silently ask the purported spirit to move the glass to a certain individual. Although unscientific and hearsay the glass will often go to the said individual thought of, and when repeated it happens again and again.

I was once fortunate enough to be one of the first individuals to investigate Burton Agnes Hall near Hull in the East Riding of Yorkshire. Built in the early 1600's Burton Agnes Hall is a stunning place filled with its fair share of ghostly stories. Sadly I must put out there that the lady who ran the event conned the owners of the building and did not pay them which was frustrating! Some psychic I am, hey! Anyway during this night, the atmosphere was electric and initially when we did some glass divination, we managed to communicate with a spirit personality called Pete. This was interesting because as the glassed moved I was able to connect with him and gain information which I could then ask to encourage the glass to move. What was impressive about this was that the guide knew exactly who this spirit entity was and the role he played in arguably the most well-known ghostly story connecting with the home. What was fascinating for me was how the guide for the evening was able to confirm the specific information I was giving which at the time was not public knowledge. It is moments like that which make you stand back as a medium and think wow! This is genuinely real!

Later on in the evening we attempted table tipping and the table I was working on had two friends I knew, another investigator and one other person. This table was relatively small and could be easily manipulated by the persons placing their hands on top; however I trusted them and doubted they would falsely manipulate phenomenon. What was fascinating about this communication was not only did we get the table rocking when communicating with a little boy; we also got knocks on the table too. These knocks were not consistent with the table leaning from one side to the other; the responses were in response to questions asked. What's more, because the table was so small you could see each individual's hands and feet thus ruling out any foul play.

As with any communication with spirit it is important you work with people who are knowledgeable, trust worthy and able to keep you safe. I would not recommend any of these techniques to try on your own or in a group that is not led by someone who has knowledge of communicating with spirit.

Part Three: Evidence from the United Kingdom and further afield.

The Scole Experiment and Marcello Bacci: Chapter Seven

There are a few spirit related matters that stand out in my mind and make me think wow! Here we have some really good evidence of spirit contact. Whilst I believe in spirit and believe in my ability to communicate I am really keen on scientific and evidence based examples of spirit communication and interaction within a controlled environment. So often examples of spirit interaction are based in pseudoscience and not properly tested - nor are they 'peer reviewed' - and as a result do not support or offer scientific evidence that the conscious mind lives on. There are many stories and personal accounts of spirit communication and whilst these do offer excellent examples of spirit interaction, they unfortunately offer limited empirical evidence which is once again testable and evidential.

I feel it my duty to explain here, one of the elements which plagues the role science has in testing mediumship and psychic phenomena. Mediumship remains on the fringes of credible scientific research and is seen by many modern scientists as nothing more than hokum and pseudo-science. I feel this is partly due to the stigma and quality of many purported psychics and mediums whose claims are not founded, and as a result leaves real practitioners reeling and ostracised.

Furthermore a wider implication relates to the general materialistic scientific paradigm in which scientists currently operate. Often science is based on the assumption that it can be tested and retested in laboratory type settings and that accurate and consistent data should be collected; when in fact mediumship is part of human nature, a psychology/sociological based phenomenon and the same rules do not apply. So how are mediums tested? Tests can be carried out in numerous ways both in a qualitative and quantitative based approach and testing the accuracy of information received by the medium. It is important to consider why such tests do not reach the public consciousness, and I would argue that the materialistic scientific paradigm in which we currently reside, is the main reason for this and rather than accepting and considering the existence of the conscious mind living on past death, there remains a dogmatic assumption that consciousness is nothing more than a chemical reaction which ceases once the body becomes no more.

Having stated the above I also sympathise with scientists and their frustration with the faulty claims made about the links between mediumship, consciousness survival and science. A good example of this is the assumption that quantum physics demonstrates that the soul lives on, when in fact there is limited evidence (at this time) to suggest this whatsoever. Whilst there may have been some experiments undertaken to test these ideas and theories regarding survival and Quantum Physics , to merely state that Quantum Physics is evidence for survival without research and evidence to back this up understandably would make scientists frustrated and further sceptical about mediumistic claims.

Within this section I wanted to highlight work being undertaken throughout the world both within the United Kingdom and predominantly Europe and the United States. For me, this is one of the most neglected areas of evidence for the survival of consciousness post life and should be more prominent in the public area, rather than the likes of *Most Haunted* and other entertainment shows.

As a result I wanted to discuss and provide an overview of the following topics:
1. The Scole Experiment

2. Electronic Voice Phenomenon
3. The Society for Psychical research- some interesting cases.
4. The Scottish society for psychical research
5. Bacci-the Italian medium
6. Evidence from medical practitioners

Within this section I hope to draw on the opinions of some of the people involved in these cases and the impact this has had on their lives and the way in which they perceive spirit communication. For me the following topics are some of the best evidence for spirit communication and what makes it good, is not some fuzzy security camera footage nor a lapsed scientific approach, but more the consistent accurate testing and data collating. Furthermore, elements of the above have been peer reviewed and stood up to this test of the scientific community.

I need to emphasise how important these pieces of work are, not only in what the evidence suggest but also the dedicated work of the practitioners involved and the personal responsibility, patience used to achieve such a high standard of communication and evidence.

The Scole Experiment

The Scole Experiment is named after the village it took place in, in the 1990's and is arguably one of the most important examples of spirit communication. It is worth noting at this point that if this actually took place and (having read the evidence and looked at the reports) I have no reason to believe not; then surely this is one of the most important scientific investigations in the history of mankind. Scole holds a special place in my heart, not only because of the dedication of the practitioners involved and the evidence collated but also because one of the lead researchers was raised in the Grimsby area, Mr Robin Foy.

The experiments were led predominantly by four individuals, Robin and Sandra Foy plus Alan and Diana Bennett. Over a number of years these four people dedicated numerous hours per week to sitting and communicating with spirit and the results their hard work gained stands out against any other modern research/physical group. It is important to return to a point raised earlier on in the book about the idea that mediumship can simply be taught in a matter of weeks, or months when in fact it takes years of dedicated practice, something which many aspiring mediums and also scientists seem to lack in their understanding of the subject. Even before Scole each of these individuals had dedicated many hours and years in their search for proof of the afterlife and development of themselves in a spiritual capacity.

It would be nearly impossible for me to do the Scole Experiment justice in the limited spacing I have in this book and much of the information I am about to share is taken from three separate sources, each well worth a read for further insight into the work at Scole and hold a worthy place on my book case at home:

Witnessing the Impossible: by Robin P Foy
The Scole Experiment: by Grant and Jane Solomen
Is There an An Afterlife? By David Fontana

A starting point for Scole perhaps is to highlight the different energies used to develop evidential phenomena, as once having established contact with the 'spirit team' the four individuals were informed that rather than traditional ectoplasm, energy only was being utilised. In fact, the spirit team were drawing on a new kind of energy which enabled them to develop phenomena differently and more creatively. Further to this not only were séances done at Scole, they were undertaken in various locations around the globe, often with the environments uncontrolled by the four main individuals and attended by up to twenty people at a time.

Although initially the phenomena started slowly, after a while it began to grow and as the trust between spirit and the group grew so did the communication and production of phenomena. The group had many varied spirits working with them and I find it interesting that the books indicate that the group may have worked with these individuals in the past, prior to Scole, suggesting that the spirit world engineered these opportunities behind the scene over an extended period of time.

Each session which was held with the spirit team was recorded, making the Scole Experiment one of the most extensively documented spirit interactions in the history of spirit communication. Perhaps before looking at the evidence achieved by the Scole Group, it is important to mention again that the group were informed early on that the group was different to traditional physical circles and that the group would be using a different energy - seemingly produced during sessions of the group from three different energy sources; one of these - spirit world energy – specially brought to earth by the spirit team each time the group sat. This was mixed with certain earth energies and the group members' own spiritual energies to form the 'creative energy' needed by the spirit team for the production of phenomena. The open minds of group members allowed them to work in different ways. Furthermore it is interesting to note that again in the early stages attempts were made to hold traditional circles and the Scole circle in the same cellar; however this proved to cause on-going problems for phenomena due to the differences in the energy and they had to be stopped. I mention this to highlight this would suggest that developing mediums/psychics need to have a good understanding of energy and how to use this to support development and how different energies interact. Unfortunately my experience is that the use of energy and how it supports spirit communication is not often discussed, or is taught inappropriately. Recently I became aware of healers working in a church where after healing, they lay on the floor to 'clear the energy'; sadly this was done within a church setting and in a public arena. Behaviour like this, in my opinion has a negative impact on the image of Spiritualism and more should be done to prevent this from happening and develop the individual's knowledge of energy.

The Scole Group had many varied forms of phenomena which consisted of traditionally based phenomena including rappings/taps, spirit communication and trumpet levitation. But it went well beyond this, including the following:

i. Apports :- Objects which were teleported into the room which held significance for the spirit communicators and were left behind after the sessions,

ii. Spirit photography:- during the experiments, over a period of time the spirit team worked to develop films initially using film in cameras, and then directly putting images on to unopened film, which (when developed) had on it various different pictures, messages and writing.

iii.   Direct spirit interaction initially through the entranced mediums but then through direct voice communication, solid spirit beings present in the room and through audio and video experiments.

There is no doubt that Scole was ground-breaking in the work it undertook and there are definitely memorable elements from the 5 year period which deserve further exploration. During the Scole Experiment they received numerous apports which were significant to the spirit communicators and at times relevant to the individuals present. One such apport is interesting due to its significance to a well-known war time medium Helen Duncan who was tried under the Witchcraft Act following investigation from the armed forces and police in war times. The case of Helen Duncan was a leading driver in the passing of the Fraudulent Mediums Act, which replaced the Witchcraft Act as she was the last person in England to be tried under the act. During one sitting, prior to the scientists' involvement, a newspaper was apported, dated April 1st 1944 which contained details relating to the trial of the physical medium Helen Duncan! What's interesting about this specific apport relates to the quality of the actual newsprint paper. Rather than being old and dated (such as might have been expected in a newspaper from 1944), it was crisp and still white rather than the usual faded yellow colour (although within days of being received it rapidly did turn yellow). One might have assumed that the paper was a modern copy requested from the publisher, but upon further forensic testing at the Print Industry Research Association , they were able to confirm that the paper was printed on original wartime paper (which due to the war at that time was made from mechanical pulp that contained the chemical lignin, but did not have certain other chemicals in it due to rationing etc) made at that time and was printed using the old fashioned letterpress process, which was no longer in operation.

Following this the group achieved significant evidence relating to spirit photography initially the spirit team used a Polaroid camera and then were able to impress their thoughts and images directly onto the films, without the use of a camera. Over time, there was opportunity to do this under scientific control, which will be touched on soon. However, what was also impressive about elements of this photography is that at times they had puzzles for the group to solve and also provided further proof of survival. It is important to highlight the work undertaken by Scole prior to the scientists becoming involved and the results they achieved with the spirit team such as some of the above; however I do want to highlight the evidence achieved using the protocols implemented by the scientists. For me personally, this bolsters the claims of the group - given their willingness to allow this to take place and invite scientists to investigate their claims.

Initially proposed by Psychologist Dr David Fontana the protocols consisted of the following four steps:

1. The investigators would bring the film to be used during the experiment,
2. During the sitting the film would be placed in a security box (independent from a camera),
3. During the sitting, the investigators would remain in control of the box,
4. Finally, the investigators would have control over the development of the film, including the equipment used.

During the testing period slight variations to the above were made, particularly to the type of container used for reasons relating to the suitability and also the possibility of fraud taking place. Whilst the scientists achieved some results using the above protocols, including some star type pictures and a German poem, the scientists were unable to achieve the same standard previously without controls in place and unfortunately were not able to conclusively demonstrate that fraud had not taken place by the group to achieve the pictures. It is important to highlight at this point, that the scientists at no stage believed the group to be tampering with the boxes or films. Unfortunately the very fact that *it (fraud) could have happened* is enough for sceptics to question the validity of the results, regardless of how small this probability would have been. Regardless of the 'limited' success (*that being perceived from a critical scientific perspective*) the scientists articulated that the results which were achieved, remain some of the best evidence to date for demonstrating the reality of survival after death.

The varying ways in which the group communicated and interacted with the spirit team is equally fascinating, not only did they communicate via the entranced mediums, they had spirit personalities projecting their voice from within the room, independent from the mediums themselves. Furthermore, they used devices developed by the spirit team themselves within the group to enhance communication through electrical devices and developed direct two way communication, reducing the need for entranced mediums. Towards the end of the experiment, this then developed into the use of a video recorder to film spirit personalities. Both on camera film and the video recordings, some of the images are fascinating - showing spirit personalities and other dimensional beings. An interesting point which I often think is overlooked regarding the Scole Experiment is the different beings the group communicated with; not only were they directly in contact with spirit beings, but also with other dimensions and worlds. This is well documented within Robin Foy's own book, which is an accurate and detailed portrayal of the work undertaken, and it is interesting to note, that throughout the contact with both spirit and other beings there remained a feeling of unconditional love and a beautiful peaceful atmosphere within the room.

During the period in which the group were sitting, they not only demonstrated to other groups around the world in different settings that were totally uncontrolled by the four members, but they were also extensively tested by scientists from the Society of Psychical Research for a two year period. I also find it interesting that they had members from the Inner Magic Circle (magicians) who attended some of the séances who have openly stated that they could not themselves reproduce elements of the phenomena demonstrated by the group by using trickery or magical tricks.

During the time the scientists spent with the group they were able to undertake tests, mainly relating to the spirit photography and achieved some good results. I also find it interesting that quite often the scientists were set abstract puzzles to solve, to further evidence the spirit team's reality. During one sitting an interesting discussion was held between one of the scientists and a spirit communicator regarding celestial bodies, which according the scientist concerned only three or four people in the country at that time would have been able to understand. Another interesting factor relating to the group was the on-going interactions with deceased eminent scientists and well known spirit people involved in helping the group achieve the phenomena with the most prominent of these being Sir Arthur Conan Doyle, Sir Oliver Lodge, Sir William Crookes, Helen Duncan and Thomas Edison, all of whom had an interest in survival during their life time.

An important point to reflect on here is the differing views regarding the role of scientists in private circles and what is the desired outcome. For the main sitters, they were convinced totally of the genuine nature of their interaction with the spirit team and were not solely focussed on providing stringent scientific proof; whilst for the scientists they continually tried to impose test conditions on the group to achieve conclusive proof of the afterlife. It is my understanding that this caused some tension during the scientists' involvement as they continued to push more tests which unfortunately the spirit team declined. The spirit team tried to accommodate many elements of the scientists' requests but often stated that their eventual intention was to demonstrate the phenomena in full light once the group had developed to that stage and as a result of this, they were then happy to liaise with the scientists further at that point.

It is interesting to explore why the scientists were not allowed to put the controls in place in order to prove survival conclusively, and my understanding is that it relates to the different objectives from both the group and the scientists. This also related to the timescale and probable impatience of the scientists to respect and acknowledge exactly how the spirit team wanted to develop. Having read articles regarding Scole and other physical mediumship groups, there is an emerging recognition amongst some scientists of understanding the dynamics of a physical circle and the wishes and feelings of both the sitters and spirit team in order to balance their requests. Whilst the scientists were unable to put in all the controls they desired, the spirit team and group were very accommodating and allowed many different tests to take place during the involvement of the Society for Psychical Research.

The scientists involved have since published a report regarding Scole which is worth a read. There have been many critics regarding the role of these scientists and the work undertaken. However they have openly challenged anyone to reproduce the phenomena (under identical circumstances) to the same degree and quality by using sleight of hand and magic tricks. To my knowledge - in almost 18 years since the end of the Scole Experiment - this challenge has never been taken up. Whilst there are discussions within the report about how some of the phenomena could be produced by non-paranormal means the scientists felt the group was genuine and were indeed communicating with the spirit world.

This is a very short and very brief summary of elements of the work undertaken by Scole and does no justice to the hard work undertaken by the individuals committed to developing spiritual communications. Furthermore I do not think it is my place to discuss how the work ended, as I hope it encourages you to explore more about the work undertaken and hopefully to develop your own opinions.

My final thoughts regarding the Scole Experiment which I feel are very important to highlight - as a reader - when coming to a decision about whether the events were real or not. The first being the need to look carefully at the facts; the books; reports and testimonies from individuals who were present. Please don't draw conclusions from sceptics on the internet, who were not there, or who have not read the relevant information. Use facts and personal judgement on which to base your opinions, rather than skewed close minded perspectives. I am not asking you to read the information and believe, more trying to encourage open mindedness and drawing logically on the evidence. If you do not believe or remain sceptical after reading the information - that is fine, at least it is based within reason. The second and closing thing I want to say about the Scole group is how committed, dedicated and focussed they were on the work they undertook and this is one of the main reasons they achieved such quality evidence. Furthermore this was developed over time, which the group understood and their patience paid off significantly. I can write with almost certainty that the people who witnessed the phenomena would have had their lives changed and at no point during the investigations did the group feel threatened or experience any negativity from the spirit world. Throughout the sessions the message from the spirit team was one of compassion for self, others and all living beings.

As, with the healing section of this book, I wanted to try and interview some of the people I have written about and again in this section I have a had the absolute pleasure of interviewing Robin Foy, regarding his views on the Scole Experiment and also his views towards the role of mediumship generally, and the underpinning role it plays in demonstrating survival after death.

Interview with Robin Foy:
Some of this has been transcribed from a Skype interview, whilst other elements have been taken directly from email liaisons.

'What are your memories of the scole experiment and the phenomenon which we witnessed?'

'It is 18 years since it finished but nevertheless it is just as fresh in my mind as if we were still there in many ways. What we witnessed was absolutely fantastic; it was ground-breaking because what our spirit team were doing was using a brand new method of communication, in that the physical mediumship and physical phenomenon that we were producing was done purely and simply with different types of energy which to our mind had not been done in a controlled way before.'

'I say that but, in fact we are aware of other groups in the world going back in many cases who were working with energy, although they weren't aware of it at the time. One of those was actually in 1926 in New Zealand in a place called Dunneham and they had a circle there with a young medium called Pearl Judd, were they got independent voice in the light, no cabinet, no ectoplasm and it was absolutely fantastic and the events were written about by a man called Paul Chapman, who was the mediums uncle called the blue room (this can be downloaded from the internet for free). It is interesting to compare their phenomenon to ours, although at the time they didn't know it was energy based (rather than ectoplasm).'

'Then going a little bit further along the line a medium called Rita Gould and she too was working with energy and no mention of

cabinets and ectoplasm and the phenomenon again was fantastic, which was pre-Scole although very similar (to Scole) she was getting full materialisation there but at that time done in a very different, which many of the spiritualist movement at the time, were doing interviews and getting it totally wrong more or hinting she was not genuine because the mediumship was not going along the lines that spiritualism understood i.e no cabinet, one deep trance and not using ectoplasm.'

'A third group which Sandra and I got involved with at the start of the Scole group in Stratford in London called the Theatre Group and that group was most definitely working with energy, and in fact we didn't even know who the medium was! It took us some time sitting there before we were able to identify the medium who was actually a French guy called Patrick who was producing all this wonderful phenomenon, they had independent voice, they had solid spirits people walking around very similar stuff to Scole in a way expect they weren't properly connected with their spirit team and unfortunately the phenomenon wasn't always controlled which wasn't a good thing but they unfortunately were not really looking towards the scientific and evidential side which was a shame, as they could have taken it a lot further.'

'Why is physical mediumship developed in the dark?'

'Good Question - which is the same as many people want to know - about physical mediumship being developed in the dark. The best answer is to liken it to the natural growth of human life! A human being is conceived in the dark; then the embryo grows in the dark and develops in the dark until - when the development is perfect and complete, the child is born into the light. Why is this so? Simply because conditions of darkness are the best natural conditions for the growth and development of a human child.'

'Exactly the same for physical mediumship. The actual aim and intention of all Spirit Teams working with GOOD, enthusiastic and committed Physical Circles is to eventually introduce their own Spirit Lighting conditions so that all phenomena can be seen and appreciated by members of - and guests at - those circles.'

'At Scole, we went a long way towards this, with amazing spirit lighting conditions - which would have improved even further if the experimental Circle had been able to continue. Physical mediums such as Kai Muegge already demonstrate their mediumship (in Kai's case mainly ectoplasmic which now includes full materialisation) in good red light (just like the photographic dark room safety lighting).'

'Many mediums attempt to demonstrate their physical mediumship before their spirit teams have been able to fully develop it to include their own spirit lighting, or been able to allow the medium/circle to include safe red lighting conditions. Sometimes this is due to the medium wishing to earn 'the mighty dollar' before there spirit team have fully developed the mediumship.'

'More and more developing physical mediums are now - however - including safe lighting in their demonstrations, as demanded by the public (with the approval of their spirit teams). It is regrettable that failing to do so gives the 'arch sceptics' a God-given opportunity to cry 'FRAUD' at such demonstrations and - in all honesty - not every physical medium that demonstrates is indeed 100% Genuine!!!'

'The phenomenon which you witnessed and saw at Scole, what stands out in your mind as the special stuff, the stuff that makes think Wow and knocks you off your feet?'

The spirit lights were very very important we got a great profusion of those, they started off as tiny little lights which would fly around the room and actually do aerobatic tricks they were properly controlled and one of the first things we got.

Then we had all the photographic work that started with thirty five mil film, that was quite amazing what was coming through on the slides (once produced) and then we started to get forty five mill film being left in their containers and once produced would be covered end to end with different photographs and communications from spirit, and that stood out with us which was quite remarkable. Then we had the video phenomenon were right at the very end we were able to get very good footage and that really knocked our socks of getting writings (on films) and through that video and film work we got a message from Thomas Edison to build a little machine (Called the TDC), which took months to get it going properly and when it was working properly we were actually speaking to other dimensions. The very first time we got it working properly the first communicator was Edison himself who spoke for fifteen minutes and that was fantastic.

There was lots of other things including levitation, were the spirit team would levitate the table right up to the ceiling and when demonstrating in California, we still had the proper layout on the table and with a crystals on the table not attached in any way and they would levitate the table, turn it on its side and spin it like a cartwheel, which was quite amazing. When it turned back upright and came back down gently none of the crystals has fallen off/moved they remained in the same place and that in itself, is quite amazing.

We also had independent spirit voice and were encouraged by the spirit team to give them (the phenomenon) different names, the spirit team wanted us to these names when working with energy so it could be separate from traditional physical mediumship ways of working. The terms were similar but we would use different names so they became energy voices but to anybody who the independent voice it had the same effect, speaking with voices in mid-air, also the very fact we had fully materialised spirit personality's in there, that was happening very regular basis, some of our guides would sometimes communicate with us and they would touch us and hold our hands. Emily (one of the main guides) was fantastic and we could anything up to 18 spirit personalities in the room at one time. The one other thing which became well known we eventually had a miniature UFO materialise in the experimental room, we use to try and call it that instead of a séance room, again to change the terms to distinguish from the traditional ways of working. The UFO on a couple of occasions went all the way round the room and sat a couple of inches from our faces so we could see it quite close up and you would see the little windows which were all lit up. Then of course, we had the people from other dimensions such as blue in the room with us and would pick our hands up and put them on his head so we *could feel that he wasn't human. But you can imagine what we felt like to be able to do that that was really quite something.*

One of things I feel which is sadly lacking in modern mediumship is trying to give evidential messages and trying to demonstrate survival and just wondered if you got any advice when working with scientist and trying to get positive results together?

'Well purely and simple once you've hot regular communication with the spirit team, you need to actually put it to them and what so many people seem to lack and seem to forget when they are demonstrating and developing mediumship is that that they don't always speak with the spirit team on an on-going basis, as though they are all working together as a combined team, such as Scole. We spoke with them and the one thing that everyone has to do is talk to the spirit team in a serious way and once you start to et full time communication with your spirit team you have to say to them: 'we are aiming to produce very evidential stuff here that will actually convince people totally of life after death and of other dimensions. What people need is a communicator such as we had Emily Bradshaw, although that wasn't her real name, every spirit personality we worked with used pseudo names, although in reality we knew who they were in most cases. Emily Bradshaw gave the most fantastic evidence each time we sat and one of the best pieces of evidence we got their related to the case of Caroline Rochester. This occurred in the early stages when we were a group of seven, and one of the sitters Bernadette, who lived in an old post office in Stansted, Essex who suspected her house was haunted and was experiencing strange things happening in the home. One day Emily came and spoke with us and said you're a little worried that your house is haunted, which Berdenatte said no, not real rather more interested their appears to be a presence there and then Emily went onto say, you've actually got a lady in your home that wants to develop healing with you. This lady and her brother were the first people to own this house and her name is Caroline Rochester and asked Bernet if she had done any investigation into the history of the home

and Emily advised them to go away and find out some more information.

So she asked her husband David to go to the local archives the following week whilst the group where seating to find out some more information, however they were unable to locate the information. Her husband then went again the week after and they actually discovered the house had been owned by a Caroline Rochester and her brother. Again this was done whilst the group were sitting so they at that point they were unaware this information had been located and Emily suddenly popped through to the group and stated your husband's now got all the information on Caroline and when the group checked the times he got that information at the same time Emily came through to the group. Throughout the experimental period there were several cases of evidential information produced by the spirit team to the members sitting. First and foremost as a group we wanted to work in a scientific way and in that we weren't really wanting spirit to come through and 'perform' and do all this wonderful different pieces, we were really putting ourselves on the line for the spirit team and allowing them to decide want they wanted to do but making them aware all the time that we wanted to get the best evidence we could get.

During the experimental period, the spirit team asked the sitters if they would be allow us to take this phenomenon as far as we can, this is all stuff we has never been done before and their fore this is pioneering work. The group agreed to this, although this is why it ultimately failed in the end because they continued to push (the work) as far as they could until they got too stopped by outside influences. When you put all the bits together it becomes pretty important stuff, some of the scientist sat with us put forward this bundle of sticks theory, which states if you have one stick and somebody criticise you, they can break that stick easily by putting out some negative thoughts or ideas, but if you have twenty different things (phenomenon) simultaneously then you put that together as a bundle of sticks it becomes very hard for the phenomenon to be disproved.'

'One of things which really frustrates me which I see quite often is that people get told by mediums or psychics that theirs

negative energies around them, or theirs bad spirits around them or theirs demons with them. Was this idea of evils spirits ever discussed with the spirit team and if so, what was their response?'

'It was never discussed because in the all the years we worked with them it never came up. I have been working circles now for forty three years and in all the time Sandra and I have been involved in this work we have never come across anything which is even partially evil. If you are working properly with the spirit and asking regularly for protection you just don't get any problems. I can honestly say that we've never come across anything evil and I have to say some of things which people come up with as evil are actually psychological and things in their own mind. If you're working on the right basis and trying to do the best for spirit and they for you will never come across anything which is a problem.'

'It is clear in your books and other things I have seen that you clearly developed strong relationships with your spirit team/guides and they became very much close friends. Do you still hear from the spirit at all in your continuing work in circles?'

'When Scole finished we were almost in complete bereavement we lost a complete family and that's exactly what it felt like. Some of them (spirit team) we have, after Scole had finished and we moved over here to Spain, in 2006 about three months afterwards we had a group from Scotland come and stay with us and quite a number of our spirit team from Scole came and spoke with us through their mediumship. Again they were working with energy and they were getting some very good stuff at that time. What we were getting from the spirit team at that point was very evidential, so yes we have had contact from quite a few people that we have worked with in the past. Over here I have helped to organise demonstrations of physical mediumship with the likes of Scott Milligan, David Thompson and with Kai Mugge. The last time we sat with David which was only three years ago we had a full materialisation of Winston Churchill actually in the room, he stamped his feet and clapped his hands to prove he was here and then said 'my name is Winston Churchill' in a voice you could not possible miss and continued by saying 'I've come

to speak with Robin Foy!' and then proceeded to have a chat with both myself and Sandra. He (Winston Churchill) has been with me for forty three years now and the sittings we have had with him have been very evidential and we still hear something from him. Although we don't get physical things happening currently, Sandra and I still sit three times a week and we still do get a certain amount of trance.'

'My book is focussed on developing mediumship and having an understanding of evidential mediumship. My final question, how has research into survival after death changed you as a person and what have you learnt when undertaking this work?'

'I been involved in a lot of circles and visited a lot of mediums, we became very friendly with Leslie Flint, we actually went to his funeral and we had twenty five/twenty six sittings with him. I started out in this in a circle in Leicester not having ever been in a circle anywhere and this just happened to be a physical circle I knew absolutely nothing about mental mediumship at that time. When I started sitting there I started researching the who area of mediumship and this being involved in this movement I have had upwards of over two hundred private sittings with mediums and out of that lot I have had so much evidence. People say to me you've had forty three years involvement in mediumship and psychical research you must know believe in life after death and I've always said to them, 'no, I don't. After all the experiences I have, I know there's life after death.' It has shown much that life does go on and there is survival after death and I have had too much evidence that I could ever deny that is the case.'

'Since you've Scole, David Fontana, Montague Keen and Arthur Ellison have passed away. David Fontana I've got a huge amount of admiration for and his works mean a great deal to me, have you heard from them since they passed over?'

'We have heard from them, but not very often.'

'Are they still actively involved in psychical research, are they helping groups from the other side?'

Yes very much so

Final thoughts on Scole........

Although the Scole group have disbanded, they independently continue work in evidencing survival, with Sandra and Robin both regular sitting in circles dedicated spirit. Alan and Diane Bennett continue to work with spirit however in a slightly different format using camera's, crystals and energy, producing some fascinating results, achieving images photographed onto the surface of crystals. I have approached the individual's working in this small group and asked them to contribute, however they declined advising they intend to publish their work in the near future.

The work of Marcello Bacci

Unfortunately work undertaken with mediumship from a scientific perspective is often solely focussed on Western English speaking countries and as a result, much of the work undertaken and published in foreign languages is not acknowledged or referenced for obvious reasons. Having said this, much of the literature regarding the spirit world which I have read would suggest that language is not a barrier and they can communicate effectively across these earthly boundaries.

Marcello Bacci, is one such individual whose work is often overlooked due to much of the publications being written in his native language, that of Italian. I first became aware of Bacci's work when researching the Scole Experiment and quickly became interested in his commitment to connecting parents with their passed children and his values surrounding the purpose of mediumship. Bacci's work is different to mainstream mediumship in that spirit communicate through an old style valve radio, with people in the room all being able to hear the spirit personalities conversing with the recipient of the message.

You may be asking, if Bacci is a medium if spirit communicate with the use of a radio, and I would argue that he is, for the following reasons. Firstly, the term medium means which is a way of communicating information and put simple, a mediums role is to act as go between, going between the sitter and the spirit personality. Again, at times you may come across mediums and psychics who do not understand this simple point, that they are not the important part of the process, they are simple a go between. Secondly, the radio does not transmit messages from spirit when Bacci is not present, which would suggest that his energies are required to make the process work.

From a scientific perspective, Bacci's work has been tested under strict scientific testing over a sustained period of time from numerous investigators including scientist from Il Laboratorio using voice technology similar to the FBI to test the genuineness of the voices, whilst also being alloed to independently check the radio and also removes elements of the radio which would allow stray radio transmissions to be misinterpreted as spirit communications.

The approached use by Marcello Bacci is called direct radio voice, a variation of the more well-known Electronic Voice Phenomenon. It has been difficult to find articles relating to Bacci's work which is partly down to the obvious language barrier, however also partly down to Bacci himself who does not regularly publicise his work. At the time of writing this, it is the authors understanding that Bacci continues to hold monthly séances open to the public were he does not charge and often does not interfere with the process opting to allow the sitters to ask questions and engage with the spirit personality's communication. Finally it is worth noting that when communicating the communicators often state they are from the world of spirit and communicates with the intent of unconditional love and wanting to prove survival after death.

The Society for Psychical Research and Qualitative Testing of Statements made by Mediums: Chapter Eight

The Society for Psychical Research is one of a number of different societies which invites members from differing scientific back grounds to discuss within a peer reviewed setting the nature of the 'paranormal', including mediumship. It is important to highlight the difference between published work which is submitted for peer review and work published in individual books. Often the work published solely in books has not been peer reviewed and can be seen more as an opinion rather than evidenced based; whereas work submitted by peer review can be tested and challenged by other professionals thus making it critical and peer reviewed by the scientific community.

This is common place within modern science and takes place across all modern scientific interests. The Large Hadron Collider in Switzerland is a good example of a style of peer review whereby two different sets of scientist have to achieve similar data in order to publish results stating they have found new particulars. Having said this, peer reviewed work comes with its own biases and issues particularly relating to paranormal research and the materialist perspectives which dogged modern day science. By this I mean that modern scientists have a structured view and set of testing which they believe should apply to testing/achieving scientific results. As a result anything which does not fit in this nice little box cannot be seen has scientifically credible despite being peer reviewed and undertaken in scientific test conditions.

I am now going to highlight one particularly study, published in the Journal for Psychical Research over three different papers from 2001 through to 2004. All in all the study undertaken was over 4/5 years long and consisted of detailed qualitative collection of data accepted by recipients of messages from mediums. Please note I have included this paper to demonstrate evidence for scientific testing of mediumship; however there are numerous papers publish arguing both for and against mediumship and the paranormal which I encourage you to read to come to your own truth.

I first became aware of the work undertaken by Tricia Robertson and Professor Archie Roy in a Scotland BBC production discussing spiritualism. The work intends to test the theory often used by sceptics: 'All mediums' statements are so general that they could apply to anyone'? Meaning can a message given by a medium to a recipient is accepted by others given the generalised contents delivered. Unfortunately my knowledge and ability to interpret the maths and formulas used within the study is limited, however I will attempt to provide an overview of the study discussing the methodology, results and conclusions drawn by the scientists involved.

The first published paper:
Robertson T.J. and Roy A.E.2001, A preliminary Study of the Acceptance by Non-Recipients of Mediums' Statements to Recipients. JSPR 65.2 91-106

The initial study consisted of the scientists taking statements delivered by mediums to specific individuals then collating this information and asking non recipients how many of the statements they could individually relate to. Initially ten mediums were involved in the study, with 44 recipients (people who received a reading) and 407 non recipients (controlled group). The statements collated during the sessions were undertaken both within public demonstrations and also within specific control groups.

Both Robertson and Roy (2001: 103) articulate the following within the paper relating acceptance of messages:

'It is a widespread belief among many of those sceptical of the existence of psychic ability that the answer to the question is 'yes'.

The first-phase study shows clearly that whatever the true explanation of the data collected by the study, the answer would appear to be 'no'.

It is interesting to note that even with a difference outcome compared to the common perspective that mediums statements are to general, the authors do not immediately assume that the reason is paranormal in nature. This is a common mistake made by supposed 'paranormal investigators' who go into an 'investigation' with the pre assumption that evidence they collect is paranormal in nature, and usually failed to explore alternative more rational explanations. During the study, attempts were made to try identifying and reduce issues relating to cultural similarities and unconscious/subconscious signs from the sitter including their appearance, age and response to question, which may influence the outcome of the study. This initial study found a higher percentage of acceptance between information accepted by the original recipient compared to the information accepted by the non-recipient.

Expanding on the above factors when I give a reading to someone I will often highlight if I have worked something out from their body language, or alternatively they've accidently given me information which I could use. Unfortunately not many mediums do this, opting to either consciously/subconsciously using the information as part of the reading. As part of development this is something every medium will go through, however it's how you use that knowledge once aware of it which is important.

I think it is important to discuss the weighing procedure used within the study, which includes the following statement:

'It is obviously desirable to have a method of weighting a statement whether or not it is accepted by the recipient. The problem is not a simple one. It is probably true that a statement such as 'you know a man called John' is nonsignificant compared with a statement such as 'I have a person here who was proud of their carefully-cultivated moustache and it is your mother! 'Yet that striking difference in weight is not the whole story. A seemingly commonplace statement may be of immense significance to the person who receives it and yet by its very ordinariness it may be capable of being accepted by many. One of the present authors

(AER) heard a medium make the statement; "I see a giant wheatsheaf in the middle of a harvested field with a man sitting on top of it and waving." Many of us have seen wheatfields and wheatsheafs, especially if we're elderly, and so we might feel obliged to accept such a statement. But to the woman to whom it was given, by a medium she had never seen before, it was emotionally shattering, for her husband had been the proprietor of the Wheatsheaf Inn.'

As a result of the initial study, the authors identified potential issues which could impact on the results produced including the above factors discussed, which they described as non-paranormal factors. Meaning that cultural differences, the recipients willingness to accept information and the mediums ability to pick up on clues could have contributed towards the large gap in acceptance between recipients and non-recipients. As a result this allowed them to amend their methodology and introduce further controls into the experiments.

The Second published paper:

Roy A.E. and T.J Robertson 2001, A Double Blind Procedure for assessing The Relevance of a Medium's Statements to a Recipient .JSPR 65.3 161-74

The second paper picks up from where the last one left on, recognising the 'potential non paranormal reasons' for the outcome of the initial findings and devised protocols which implemented the following steps:

- the medium and recipient are hidden from each other's view;

- the recipient does not speak to the medium;

- the recipient does not know he is the recipient;

- the medium cannot identify the recipient in any normal way;

- each of the other participants is unaware of whether he is the recipient
or a *non-recipient;*

- neither of the two investigators chooses the recipient.

Although no result are published within this paper, it does discuss in detail some of the queries raised regarding the protocols in the first study and how they have amended the methodology to account for non-paranormal means for differences in the results.

The third paper:

Robertson T.J. and Roy A.E. 2004, Results of the Application of the Robertson-Roy Protocol to a series of Experiments with Mediums and Participants. JSPR 68.1 18-34

The paper goes in depth with regard to the outcome of the whole study and the painstaking work which was undertaken to arrange the study through to collecting the data. Again my limited understanding of data analysis and mathematics does not allow me to give a synopsis of how the information was collected and evidenced; however the findings do show that even with appropriate protocols in place relating to controlled environments and weighing of information provided by mediums; that the third paper shows that after the second phase of experimentation that hypothesis was nullified with the odds against chance being a million to one.

The reason for discussing this paper is not only the findings but also the process for how the information was collected and developed. Not only did the authors address issues relating to information collated through non paranormal means, they also tried to address issues relating to queries raised by other scientists. This includes amending the protocols involved in the experiment and tighten the testing criteria relating to the initial question asked. Furthermore, they published their work over a period of time, which enabled it to peer reviewed and document their progress.

I remember watching the BCC documentary about the experiments in which one the mediums made statements such as: 'This person lives at Christmas Cottage', which when checked with the recipient of the message was factually correct. Now to put that into context given the protocols develop and methodology used, the probability of such statements being made must be high.

Unfortunately one of the authors of the papers Archie Roy has passed away, however his contribution to mediumship and survival after death is impressive and no doubt his works and writings will continue to prove valuable to future researchers.

As a result of writing about the above study, I have been fortunate to make contact with one of the authors Tricia Robertson. Tricia is a well-respected researcher of survival of life after death and her appearance in T.V documentaries and presentations speaks volumes relating to her knowledge on the subject. As a result please find a short interview I was able to hold with Tricia relating to her wider studies of life after death and some of her experiences thus far:

My first question relates to the five year of mediumship you undertook, what did you learn following that study, and did it change your view mediumship and survival after death?

Our research that Archie Roy and I did, we spent five years studying mediumship information, that being information passed on from a medium to a recipient. We all know the sceptics are quite right, if you're sitting in a an audience and you (the medium) can see someone sitting there, first of all you know whether if it's a man or a women, roughly what age they are and however hard you try as a medium, you make suppositions about that person. We all do this when we meet someone we immediately make suppositions about them, sublimely we does this and this is a fact.

So we set up this experiments which ranged up to triple blind experiments were the medium cannot see the audience, that the audience cannot see the medium, therefore the medium does not know who the recipient is, man or women. In the majority of cases the recipients did not know they were the receiver of the said message received from the medium. So it took us five years to figure this all out and get it honed perfectly where I would in a another room, with a medium that Archie Roy wouldn't even see and we would have a microphone going from the medium into the hall where the recipients sat, so they could hear the medium speak but the medium could not see the responses from the people sat in the room. It was more complicated than this, but this is the basic premise of the experiments and it in essence the medium did not have contact with the recipients, nor could get clues from bodily language or other responses.

You know as a medium if you say to someone 'I have your father here', they nod automatically or give you a clue that you're on the right track. After a long five years of study with this complicated strict protocol, in fact we wouldn't even know who the recipients were, because we use to do it by numbering the sits randomly in the hall. When people came in they were given seat numbers randomly and chosen by themselves upon entering, so they had to sit on randomly selected sits. When we did it in Edinburgh we put an advert out in the local paper requesting people to attend so this was totally out of our control, including that of the medium.

After five years the hypothesis we were testing was 'that all mediums statements are so generally that they could apply to anyone', because this is what the sceptics say. I have to say in a lot of cases sadly this is true, there is a lot of crap going about in mediumship. Unfortunately nowadays we are looking for people who want to be famous or want to make money out of it. It is not a money making exercise and certainly psychical research is not a money making exercise, I wouldn't like to think of the money Ive spent over the last 32 years, I chose to do this in the pursuit of truth. Now here we come to your first question, after the research we showed using good mediums, that the hypothesis being tested that statements are to generally was nullified, to the degree of one million to one, meaning the odds against our result being chance we a million to one. This was calculated from all the data we took, if we cherry picked the best of the mediums, it would have been much more than that; it would have been 10 to the minus 12 against chance!

A million to one is still very good odds, now all that shows is that good mediums can deliver meaningful information to a recipient with odds against a million to one. But remember were only talking about information, for example 'I've got your father here, his name is Joseph, he had red hair, he worked at such a place', the medium is making statements, that information being passed on in statements , but it doesn't prove survival. All this shows is that a medium can gain information about a recipients outside of the 'normal parameters'. In most the medium doesn't know where they get the information from, as a medium you don't, you just know you get information. I remember twenty years ago to Gordon Smith saying to Gordon Smith 'where do you think you get the information from?' and he said *'sometimes I get it at the side, from the top of my head, sometimes from the floor, I just get the information.'* A lot of mediums don't really know where they get the information from.

This leads us to the idea of a collective consciousness and it goes back to the idea of the akashic records, everything we say and do is documented somewhere for ever, and in our day and age we can understand better as some digital archive. I'm not religious; I am not Christian I'm not anything, more and more when you think about it, even in the bible it says the very hairs on your head are numbered. And you now I think that is right, I think that has to be correct, every single thing that happens, is documented somewhere like in a cosmic archive. Now arguably that archive can be accessed by some mediums and that is what we call a psychic reading I think, you're taping into the archive, say you're talking to a person and somehow you can type into the archive of his life. This does not prove survival, but when you get things like drop in communicators, when people spirits are coming in and you're not asking them to come and you don't know the spirits and their giving you information that nobody in the whole place knows that a different thing entirely. That's when you begin to think there's more to it and of course the best of all is when they give information which then recipients has to go away and check and find out if it is correct and if the information provided happened after the spirit person died, them that is even better, If your archive closes after you die, then the spirit person would arguably not know this.

And of there are so many very personal messages that you're in doubt that it is an actually person speaking, with its personality and all its traits giving you that information. And this is the whole problem, theirs such a range of information that you get from mediums and quite frankly I think, if we're lucky only twenty percent of the mediums in the whole UK are any good! Thiers such a lot mediocre mediums and theirs downright rubbishy mediums as well, but there are the gold stars, and they don't necessarily need to be the big names, we got one in Edinburgh just now called Barry Hogg is very East Coast he talks away in Scottish dialect, I have trouble understanding, he can produce the most amazing information, unusually information. I heard one says to a girl near me the first thing he said was *'you knew somebody* that took a horse to a pub?' and she responded saying 'yes!' and he said 'Really?' and you knew somebody that ran away from a circus, with the girl saying 'it was the same man' he continued and said 'this can't be right, he said somebody is telling me you took a pet bird wrap it in tin foil and put it in the freezer?' and she said ' yes that is right as well!' This are not things you can guess easily, and there was a reason for that message her partner was away at the time and they had a pair of love birds and the lady bird died but she didn't want to do anything with it whilst he was away so she wrapped it up and popped in in the freezer. These statements are things we had done in the here and now which the spirit person communicating could not have known about, because they were dead before they happened. These are the things that keep me going.

As you previously discussed, the Electronic voice phenomenon, is something I would like to look into myself at some point because the Italian Marchello Bacci, produces some great stuff and Anabella Cordoso, and she seems to get some interesting result and my friend Professor David Fontana he was very convinced by Electronic Voice Production and of course, that would be the gold standard, the voice comes right through and there's no personality of the medium there. It is all incredible complicated the more you go into it and as far as I am concerned mediumship is only one way to look at survival theirs all this other ways as well. Then you get to the likes of their crash of the R101, when you've all the people coming through from spirit giving details of what happened to them and what happened to the 101. The engineer telling engineering information, the structural engineer could tell you something else, the radio engineer giving different information; in fact I think the crash of the R101 is one of the best cases ever for proof of survival. If you need the airmen that would not die, the British Government made errors with the air ship and because of the efforts to complete this, the vehicle was totally unsuitable for purpose. And that is why is Erwin came through, and said 'were all murderers, were all bloody murderers' and they laid the blame squarely on the government. The technical information given was accurate and factual.

To close on the question you originally asked, the research at first doesn't tell me anything about the afterlife, it only tells me that good mediums can in part good/relevant information to sitters. It is only when you get really specific information for the sitter after that person has died and something that the sitter doesn't know and has to go away and check then we can really start to consider survival.

Mediumship research…what it tells us

Research with good mediums exhibits the fact that these mediums can access and impart relevant information to recipients. Information that they could not possibly have gained knowledge of by any normally accepted means.
Certainly telepathy exists, experiments clearly show this.
Some people may like to label mediumship as telepathy, but no……no telepathy experiments have ever produced the detail and quantity of information provided by good mediums.
In my joint 5 year mediumship research and experimentation programme with Professor Archie Roy, the odds against our results being due to chance were a million to one, even under the strictest of protocols.
Thus showing that under experimental conditions mediums were providing relevant information to recipients about deceased personalities. This, however, does not really prove survival of those personalities, just that mediums can access information about those lives….. Something in itself which is extraordinary.
However mediums can provide information in way which exhibits the knowledge and personality of a deceased person in such a manner that the identity of that person seems beyond reasonable doubt. This is particularly true when the person receiving the information has to subsequently check out the information given and it is later found to be correct.
There are so many examples of this, but I cite the R101 disaster and Murder most foul in my books as two of them.

Advice to developing mediums…… be very careful who you sit with for development, always keep a sense of humour and your feet on the ground. You are only a medium as long at discarnate personalities come through you. You do not have any power. Take a long time to develop and do it properly.

Why does mediumship and paranormal research continues to marginalised by mainstream science?

Unlike my colleague Professor Archie Roy, a lot of scientist don't want to come out saying they believe either because of religion within science or because they lose credibility, scientist can lose tenure at a university etc. It is only the brave ones that come out, but this is changing because Professor Benard Carr who's an Astronomer and Astrophysicist a friend of mine says that physics allows for that, for things such as different dimensions, as does Quantum Physics. With regard to studying the paranormal, Science is starting to come into its own, more and more scientist are testing people in laboratories and seeing there are differences.

There is a Brazilian medium Chico Xavier who could do automatic writing and he was mediumistic, doing wonderful things for the Brazlian people through his gif. His Brain waves were monitored when he was in a relax state and then again when he was demonstrating his mediumship via automatic writing. These were than tested in a laboratory and the brain waves, were markedly different which would indicate there is something happening in the brain when demonstrating mediumship. For me this is great, evidence that something different happens to your brain when demonstrating genuine mediumship. That is important, that is something you can hang your hat on, something pragmatic. Northampton University are undertaking research with mediums at Standstead Hall, they have pads which they place on the medium and they monitor and download information which they can analysis the mechanics of mediumship. Thiers nothing better when a good medium gives reliable information to an individual who is grieving, even when I am giving a talk there is someone sitting in that room, that's had a broken heart. Mediumship and discussions on survival should be done respectfully and difficultly.

The Cardiff Poltergeist: Chapter Nine

In the next section I want to look at some more investigative work undertaken in collaboration with the Society for Psychical Research, and again with David Fontana. I remember well the time as an adult I came across this case as I instantly remembered fondly watching an episode of *strange but true* about 11 years of age and being really scared yet unable to tear my eyes away from the screen.

Before discussing this case in a little more detail it is probably a good time to discuss Poltergeist in general and some of the myths, confusion and fear associated with the word. The word 'Poltergeist' comes from the roughly translated German word meaning noisy ghost/spirit and entered the general public consciousness with the release of Spielberg's now classic Poltergeist film in the early 1980's.

Throughout this book I have articulated my view that much of what I write about is my own interpretation. I encourage you to find your own understanding with many aspects of this book and survival after death in order for you to come to your own truth. However even within the spiritual community and ghost hunting groups alike there is widespread disagreement about what a poltergeist actually is. Some believe it to be associated with spirits that manipulate the energy around people and cause mischief and thrive off fear. Whilst others believe that poltergeist phenomenon is a form of energy created by a human conduit and the phenomenon is created or influenced by human emotions. My own belief is that this phenomenon in most instances is misunderstood and influenced by our own limited understanding of the unseen world around us. Despite this I will also present cases where there are elements of spirit related activity associated with it, such as the Cardiff Poltergeist and the Enfield Haunting.

Let's face it! In most cases fear sells, whether this is in books, films or events most people enjoy to a more or lesser degree being scared and get a sense of excitement from this. Unfortunately this is the situation with the idea of poltergeist and ghost in general. Unfortunately *some* within the spiritual community are more interested in 'acting' as individuals who are experts in dealing with such things, when in fact they have a blinkered and limited understanding and arguably take advantage of vulnerable individuals. So often I come across supposed mediums and ghost hunting groups who purport to be able to deal with such negative forces and it is not uncommon for me to hear these same people tell the public they have (supposed) negative energies in their homes. Contrary to the popular misconception about 'supposed' negative manifestations, true poltergeist phenomenon is rare, often time limited and has a number of common factors including the following:

i) the phenomenon usually starts unexpectedly usually with none of the family members experiencing similar events prior

ii) the phenomenon is often time limited and dependent upon the circumstances can last for a period of weeks or a number of years

iii) There are general two types of poltergeist phenomenon, the first is often centred on an individual (an agent) usually a young child going through puberty and the phenomenon is described a psychokinetic and caused by biological and physiological changes within the body and how this interacts with the environment around the person. The second type can be spirit interaction and is arguably the more common type.

The first type- Psychokinetic

Often when people have a 'paranormal experience' it is usually unexpected, sporadic and scary for those that witness it, this is especially true if you see an object fall of a shelf or something moves in the property. Immediately our natural instinct comes to the fore front of our minds and we begin to think of scary monsters out to possess and control us! This unfortunate view as discussed above is part of the mainstream misunderstanding of such events. Over the years I have had the opportunity to demystify this belief, partly through experience but also down to research and looking at it from a perspective of reasons rather than fear.

Quite typically poltergeist cases are centred on a person, described technically as the poltergeist agent. Being different from a traditional haunting, the phenomenon is centred on the agent rather than a property and usually follows the individual about. Often the agent is an younger person such as an individual going through puberty or experiencing high levels of emotional stress and unable to challenge these feelings in a perceived normal manner. As a result the agent experiences a build-up of emotional energy both consciously and subconsciously which results in this psychokinetic energy being created and phenomenon occurring as a result.

Often the phenomenon is uncontrolled, sporadic and includes the following:
i) Electronic devices failing
ii) Items falling of shelfs/flying about
iii) Possessions bursting into flames
iv) Heavy furniture moving
v) Knocks and bangs being heard around the home
vi) Stones falling from mid-air, without a source being located

Poltergeist cases have been described in literature for centuries with records dating back to the 1600's and what is interested about these descriptions, is that the phenomenon is often the same, and follows a similar pattern. This is interesting as these accounts come from different countries over a number of years, and usually independent from each other, thus strengthening the case for the phenomenon being witnessed as genuine.

Despite years of investigation, their remains scepticism regarding poltergeist activity and even amongst the believers of such phenomenon their remains lack of clarity about how this phenomenon is created by human agents. This partly down to the material reductionist perspectives within modern science but also due to the unpredictability of when and where the phenomenon may occur, thus making it incredible difficult to study consistently. Sceptics often state that the phenomenon is fraudulent in nature, or the event witnessed by researchers has been carelessly observed. Despite this, there are cases which have been observed by numerous different people including members of the public, police and experts in the study of psychical and paranormal research. Furthermore there has been cases whereby elements of the poltergeist phenomenon has been tested in laboratories including the acoustic noises produced by the raps which produce a different noise compared to a non-paranormal rap.

To summarise the above section, poltergeist phenomenon is not always caused by unseen spirits wanting to cause trouble, more often than not the phenomenon witness has a central focus point such as an agent and interlinks somehow with the agents emotional state. The study of such cases isn't always straight forward and there can be overlaps between poltergeist cases and traditional haunting type phenomenon.

The second type

As explained above it is my belief that much poltergeist phenomenon is misunderstood, however there are cases whereby there appears to be an overlap with some presenting phenomenon and spirit related activity. It is interesting to note that agents who experience events such as described may also be more open and receptive to spirit and psychic events. As a result, poltergeist events could lead to spirits being present within the home and this becoming confused and blamed on spirit rather than the agent.

There may also be times when spirits are responsible for phenomenon and whilst objects may move, this is not poltergeist in nature. Often during readings I have found that spirit tell me they have either left something in the property such as a feather, or alternatively they have moved something like a photo or interfered with an electronic item. This is often done not to scare but to prove they have been around the individual and watching over them, this is not done to cause fear more to demonstrate survival. Another important difference between these two types is the evidence spirit related poltergeist phenomenon provides for supporting the idea of survival after death. By this I mean, if a living person can get a response and communicate with the poltergeist this would support the argument for survival of the conscious mind after bodily death.

Cardiff Poltergeist Case

With regard to this second type I now want to discuss a case of poltergeist related activity which demonstrates the second type of phenomenon. This case dates back to the 1980's and much of the phenomenon witnessed centred around a small business called Mower Services owned/run by John Matthews, his wife Pat and Fred Matthews. Records indicate the phenomenon started one day when John and Fred were working in the workshop when they heard a loud bang and clattering on the roof which they thought was a result of children being mischievous. John went outside to investigate and to his surprise could not find anyone nearby or in the grounds of the business, however upon returning to the workshop the noises began again much to the surprise of the brothers.

What followed was an intense period of phenomenon witnessed by numerous individuals including Police, Insurance officials and members of the public, including customers visiting the store. Records indicate that the neither of John or Fred felt scared by the presence being there and even nicknamed him 'Pete the Poltergeist'. Pete the Poltergeist produced many different types of phenomenon during his stay including money/keys disappearing and reappearing, objects being thrown, responses to moods of staff. Most importantly with regards to this case, Pete appeared to respond intelligently to questions asked and would respond appropriately either through tapped responses or by throwing objects such as stones at specific point in the workshop. Phenomenon such as this is important as it builds evidence for intelligent communication post death which would supports the idea of survival research, rather than psychokinetic energy which remains a dominant discourse in modern parapsychological thinking.

This case was studied methodically by the *Society for Psychical Research* (SPR) and lead investigator Psychologist David Fontana. You can find a more detailed report on this case in David Fontana's books: *'is there an afterlife?'* and some of the information used within this next section is taken from his writings on his own experiences. The owners of the store contacted the SPR after experiencing two years of phenomenon within the store and following advice from a local minister and concerns that a customer might get injured they decided they needed further advice. During the first visit to the store, David Fontana reports that upon walking into the workshop he was greeted by the sound of a stone pinging off a metal object, with the owner commenting that the poltergeist was welcoming David into the store.

During this initial visit to the lawn mower shop, David established that the phenomenon started two years prior in 1987 when John and his colleague were watching television one afternoon when large stones began to be thrown onto a large metal roof. They became baffled as they believed the stone throwing was a result of children, even to the extent they called the Police to catch the suspected culprits. Over the subsequent months, the phenomenon increased and owners began to experience things within the workshop including:-

1) Stones
2) Bolts
3) Coins
4) Older coins (dated 1912)
5) Tools swinging on the racks
6) A blue flame emerging from a ornament brass shell case which at times would be thrown violently across the room
7) Planks of wood reported to be too heavy to lifted by hand thrown through the open workshop door
8) Dust being dropped down the collar of individuals working at the shop
9) And frequent movement of carburettors used in the lawn mowers being moved/thrown about

The poltergeist would also produce phenomenon in the home of John and Pat and another couple who worked in the shop. Interestingly on this point, it is my understanding that the second couple have remained anonymous which is not uncommon when people report paranormal occurrences. Often they fear ridicule and fear being mocked for believing in such phenomena, yet this in itself supports the genuineness of such events and goes against the sceptics argument that people reporting paranormal events are looking for fame or attention. Within his book, David Fontana highlights that during his investigations of the reported poltergeist events, none of the individuals involved (apart from one individual, who had one previous experiences) had experienced any paranormal occurrences prior to the events in the workshop and appeared genuine, honest individuals whose accounts of the phenomenon tallied and were consistent in nature.

It is interesting that at times, the poltergeist would make attempts to be helpful, for example if work was being undertaken on a lawnmower, one of the engineers would mention he needed a part and this would unexpectedly drop out of the air. Furthermore, there were reports that John would open the workshop some mornings and in the kitchen area attempts to lay breakfast cutlery had been undertaken. At times, John would set tests for Pete in attempts to try and prove the phenomenon to be real. This included one evening leaving a carburettor placed on a unlit gas heater in the workshop with John encouraging Pete to move it upon him being the last one to leave the workshop, locking up for the night and heading home. It is reported that on the way home, John's colleague felt a sharp prick in his hand when getting change out of his pocket, only to be confronted with a carburettor in his hand. It is further reported that John and his colleague upon realising this return to the store and found the carburettor left on the gas heater to be missing.

One day John became frustrated with the continuing phenomenon, suspecting that it was a prank by his work colleagues he arranged for them to stay behind after closing time and test if the stone throwing continued. All three placed their hands in view on the counter and the stone throwing did continue, with one of the work colleagues suggesting they ask for specific tools to be bought. It is reported that as they asked for the specific tools they fell from thin air materialising in front of them, arriving with such speed that John reported he could not find the tools that quickly himself. David Fontana states within his book that this specific event John witnessed is what convinced him that the events were in fact genuine.

Other 'tests' which were carried out by the proprietors of the store and at times with David Fontana present included – throwing stones into a corner of the workshop and experiencing stones being thrown back at them. This occurred one day when John again became frustrated with the stone throwing and threw one back at a corner of the room where much of the phenomenon appeared to emanate from. Further experiments included asking Pete to throw stones at specific objects including a souvenir 25 pounds brass WW2 shell which Pete successfully achieved. The phenomenon was varied and whilst the investigation did not yield communication with Pete via the traditional form of asking they did achieve some level of interaction. Once the group of individual's playfully asked for money to arrive and three pennies dating from 1912 where found in the workshop, then upon asking for some more, crumpled five notes began materialising in and around the workshop.

David Fontana discusses within his book that over time as he witnessed the phenomenon taking place he became increasingly convinced and once whilst John and the others where away on holiday he experienced phenomenon independently within the workshop thus ruling out any reservations he may have had that the phenomenon was staged by the group (Not that he believed that to be the case at all, in fact describing the main participates of the study as honest, friendly and relaxed).

The Cardiff Poltergeist case is one of many which offers strong evidence for survival after research, and furthermore is a case which isn't shrouded in controversy such as the better known cases like the Enfield poltergeist and many reported American cases.

The Enfield Poltergeist Case

The Enfield Poltergeist case is one of the better known cases of poltergeist activity and has gained notoriety over the years, due to questions regarding the genuineness of the phenomenon. The Enfield case has recently been made into a feature film The Conjuring 2, which is loosely based on the actually events.

The Enfield haunting started in the 1977 and was centred on the Hodgson family, a working class single parent family. Whilst initially focussed on the family as the phenomenon continued it started to be centred around 11 year old Janet, one of the daughters. The events started one evening when Janet and her younger brother Johnny heard shuffling in their room when going to bed. Their mother Peggy convinced it was the children acting up went upstairs to ask them to quieten down. Upon leaving the room the sounds began again and a chest of drawers moved across the room. At this point Peggy returned into the room to tell Janet and Johnny off and she witnessed the chest of drawers moved aggressively towards her.

Peggy made attempts to move the chest of drawers back and initially was able to, however upon trying again to move it back into position she was unable to push it. As a result Peggy and the children decided to go downstairs, somewhat unnerved by their experiences. It is at this point that the knocking started in the property and Peggy became convinced that there were intruders in the house. She contacted her neighbours who helped searched the property but found nothing.

The Police were also called and whilst at the property WPC Carolyn Heeps, reported seeing a chair rise up and move across the floor by its own volition. This was witnessed by Police, neighbours and the family, all who were astounded by what they had seen. As the occurring events were not a Police matter and unable to help the family, WPC Heeps made a decision to contact the Daily Mail who arranged to visit the house. When at the property the reporters found nothing out of the ordinary and upon leaving and walking towards their car, they were called back into the house. Upon entering the living room they witnessed Lego bricks and marbles floating around the room, with a Lego brick hitting one of the reporters hard just above the eye.

The reporters made a decision to contact the Society for Psychical Research and sent two investigators, initially Maurice Grosse and then to support Guy Lyon Playfair a researcher specialising in Poltergeist cases. It was not long before Grosse and Playfair started to witness strange events occurring in the home, similar to that witness by others prior. Over the next few months Grosse and Playfair witnessed items being thrown, tipped and floating within the home including: furniture, coins dropping out of thin air and probably at this point the most random phenomenon of a dog barking, without a dog being present in the property.

Other phenomena targeted Janet and her sister Rose where they would be thrown from their beds or be grabbed by unseen hands. On one occasion the investigators made a decision to remove everything from Janet's bedroom to see how the poltergeist would respond. Later on in the evening the family heard a loud wrenching metallic sound coming from Janet's bedroom and as they entered they discovered the iron fireplace had been pulled out of the wall.

The evidence so far sounds compelling and at the very least frightening for those involved. The case took a sinister twist when Janet started to enter trance like states and a male voice could be heard communicating. Upon communication being established the voice indicated that he was a previous resident of the property a Bill Wilkins. The supposed spirit communicating was able to provide specific details regarding his death including that he went blind prior to passing and had a brain haemorrhage whilst sat in his living chair. The investigators where even able to verify elements of his personality and demeanour at a later date by playing recordings of the voice to Bill Wilkins son whom agreed and believed it was his father communicating.

It is interesting to note that whilst happening Janet was clearly scared and struggled to understand the voice; in later interviews stated her belief that she felt the poltergeist was not evil, more wanting to be part of the family and laid to rest.

Whilst compelling the Enfield Poltergeist is not without its critics and questions regarding the validity of the phenomenon recorded. This centred on times where Janet and her sister were caught cheating either throwing themselves about the room or on one occasion being caught by two other SPR researchers bending spoons. Janet has been open in interview since confirming that at times they did cheat partly due to being children, but also due to pressure and expectations of others for phenomenon to be achieved. However this does not negate from the fact independent witnesses objectively observed phenomenon away from the children. Consideration also needs to be given to the level of detail Janet provided when the spirit of Bill Wilkins purportedly communicated through her regarding the details of his death in the home. It is impossible for me to cover the whole events at Enfield in any detail within this book and this barely scratches the surface regarding the events and phenomenon.

As with many high profile paranormal related cases in the mainstream media the Enfield Poltergeist case continues to divide believers and sceptics alike. At the very heart of this case it ultimately demonstrates the difficulties in gathering scientific evidence away from laboratories which is critical and analytical in nature. Interestedly enough, even with all the criticism and cynicism towards the case, the SPR have since reviewed the findings and backed the evidence purporting it demonstrates evidence of paranormal powers.

Something Strange afoot: Chapter Ten

The Works of Leslie Flint

Much of today's mediumship is the mental type particularly being demonstrated in spiritual churches, halls and on Television across England, Europe and around the world. Then there are those who opt to develop physical mediumship either in secret or with limited public access. In reality it is difficult to truly gain accurate pictures of how many of these groups are sitting and if they are producing or experiencing regular physical phenomenon. Physical mediumship over the last 100 – 150 years has steadily declined, especially after the heights of the Victoria era and World Wars with the likes of Scottish medium Helen Duncan. Sadly this decline has led to many sceptics to argue that physical mediumship was nothing more than trickery, or practitioners deceiving gullible individuals into believing their loved ones lived on.

Despite this view there is a wealth of evidence historically and present which argues against this, mediums that have been tested by learned individuals with a sound understanding of the importance of being rational, logically and not easily deceived. The argument put forward that scientist from the turn of the 20th century lacked the skills to test physical mediumship is also flawed given that one of the greatest scientist in history, Albert Einstein's theory of relativity continues to stand the test of time even today over a 100 years on. Even Einstein pondered the concept of a universe created by a force not understood within the parameters of our current understanding of science:

'Everyone who is seriously involved in the pursuit of science becomes convinced that a spirit is manifest in the laws of the Universe-a spirit vastly superior to that of man, and one in the face of which we with our modest powers must feel humble.'

We have touched on physical mediumship demonstrated at Scole, within 'traditional circles' and also the likes of Marcello Bacci and his valve radio. Leslie Flint was unique with his gift and the way it manifested. Born in Hackney, London he came from a typical working class background and throughout his life suffered with ill health. Flint became aware of his gift early on, and the spirit world became a part of his everyday life. Flint set up a circle in the London area to demonstrate his gift and quickly his unique skill became well known.

What made Flint unique? Flint's mediumistic gift was different to traditional forms of mediumship and his skill developed into a form of mediumship called Independent Direct Voice. This is an abstract from the Official Leslie Flint website:

'The process is activated by Spirit communicators and their voices can be almost identical to the way they sounded on Earth,

Depending on the strength and available energy, Spirit may be able to build an ectoplasmic voice box in mid-air.

Their voices are entirely independent of the Medium and can be heard by all present. This is quite different from spirit who speak through the larynx of an entranced medium or channel.'

Leslie Flint would often sit in the dark with his sitters and providing the conditions were right, voices would talk around him, often more than one conversing with individuals present. Although sitting in the dark, Flint used no paraphernalia such as trumpets and was awake throughout the whole proceedings. At times Leslie Flint could also be heard conversing with the voices and sitters alike, at the same time the voices could be heard.

During his time Flint's mediumistic skills enabled numerous spirits to communicate, including famous spirit personalities such as Rudolph Valentino, Actor Leslie Howard, Composer Ivor Novello, the Arch Bishop of Canterbury Cosmo Lang and Her Majesty Queen Victoria. This later led to Flint being invited to have tea at Kensington Palace with Victoria's daughter Princess Louise. It is interesting to note that regular communicators would demonstrate and discuss the evolution of their souls within the spirit world. Over time they became wiser and more aware of the development of spirit both within the spirit world, but also humans/animals on the Earth plain.

'I do my work by sitting wide awake in total darkness with other people. I know I have learned more about life, people and human problems and emotions, by sitting in the dark, than I could possibly have learned in any other way – and those who have taught the most, are people dead to this – but who are living in the next.' (Leslie Flint)

Flint was no stranger to having his mediumship tested by scientist of the day and he endured a wide range of different experiments. These included being bound and gagged in a chair, through to holding a specific amount of water in his mouth for the entire séance. Flint even permitted microphones to be used to record his larynx to ensure that he was not using a form of ventriloquism, but still the voices kept flowing.

Throughout the time Flint demonstrated his rare gift, the voices continued to stress the importance of spiritual development both on the Earth Plain and in spirit, whilst also continually spreading the message of unconditional love and the need to care for people in this Earthly life. Throughout his years as a public speaking medium Flint didn't do it for money, often declining offers from people to pay for sittings. Much of Flints work is available on line and can be listened to on YouTube for free also there are a number of books published about his life and work which are definitely worth further exploration.

Electronic Voice Phenomenon

Staying on the subject of voices from the spirit world I now want to move onto the subject of Electronic Voice Phenomenon, more commonly known as EVP. Sadly much of the electronic voice seen by the wider public is the poor pseudoscience published by paranormal groups using the wrong equipment and little scientific parameters. Despite this, there is credible work being undertaken in this area, but first what is EVP and how does it work?

Essentially EVP is a way to communicate with spirit, by recording them on electronic devices (often voice recorders) with researchers believing that the spirit voices can be caught on tap and played back for people to hear. The most common way of these voices being captured is by playing white noise from a radio and then filtering out the sound to hear a specific voice, often these voice recordings are fast and last for less than two seconds. Whilst often hard to hear and interpret, EVP's are usually picked up with specialist or sensitive equipment by professionals committed to regular EVP sittings. During my time studying mediumship I have also come to understand there are times when spirits randomly choose communicate with family members and others via all sorts of electrical devices including telephones, televisions and believe or not fax machines!

There remains controversy regarding EVP's as often they are short, difficult to interpret, difficult to hear and it is argued that the voices are nothing more than stray radio transmissions picked up from radios or passing taxi's and emergency vehicles. Despite this, there is evidence to suggest that when some controls are put in place, responses can be gleaned from direct questions and the answers often correlate to the questioned posed. With commitment and the right equipment, results can be achieved within a relatively short period of time, including the use of meditation, regular set times and actively listening to the responses.

EVP's can be categorised into three different types as defined below:-

- Class C: Characterized by excessive warping. They are the lowest in volume (often whispering) and are the hardest to understand.

- Class B: Usually characterized by warping of the voice in certain syllables. Lower in volume or more distant sounding than Class A. Class B is the most common type of EVP.

- Class A: Easily understood by almost anyone with little or no dispute. These are also usually the loudest EVPs.

Some of the earliest pioneers of electronic voice phenomenon include the likes of Jürgenson and Raudive during the 1950's. Friedrich Jürgenson first became interested in voices from beyond the grave when out recording wild birds and upon reviewing the tapes he heard voices, which he recognised including the voice of his deceased father and late wife calling his name. This spurred on Jürgenson to explore the phenomenon further and eventually become convinced that the voices he had heard were genuine. Jürgenson is considered the 'father of evp' and later went on to record voices using a reel to reel recorder and went on to work with Raudive.

Raudive a fellow Swede became fascinated by the work of Jürgenson and sent about making his attempts to record electronic voice, going on to record numerous voices, employing electronic engineers to perfect the recording techniques and went on to publish manuscripts on his findings. Interestingly Raudive recorded voices in an RF – Screened Laboratory, essentially a room blocking outside radio frequency. Raudive further set up experiments to test the quality of his recordings by inviting people to listen and interpret what they heard. It is reported on the day of his funeral Jürgenson showed himself on the television set of a former colleague which he was able to take a photograph of, well over 200 miles away from where the funeral was taking place.

In the late 70's early 80's Martin O'Niell and George Meek developed a machine called Spiricom a set of 13 tone generators spanning the sound of the human voice. O'Niell a physical medium and George Meek developed the machine following communications from the spirit world and after months of developing the large radio like apparatus they began to hear the voice of a spirit individual in an electronic/robotic like voice. This voice announced itself as the deceased scientist Dr George Jeffries Mueller a college physics teacher informing the pair he had returned to assist them in developing a direct communication with spirit. The pair in conjunction with the deceased Mueller went on to record over twenty hours of recordings between 1979 and 1982.

The pair later went on to publish the design specification and encourage other practitioners to develop the machine, however my understanding is that no one since has been able to replicate the phenomenon something which Meek puts down to O'Niells physical mediumship skills. The recordings themselves are widely available on the internet to listen to, whilst I am slightly sceptical given that others have not been able to produce the same phenomenon independently nevertheless they are fascinating to listen too.

EVP recordings continue to be collected today by a wide range of people from individuals interested in the phenomenon, through to grieving parents and scientists alike. From the likes of Dr Annabelle Cardoso through to the Association of Transcommunication there are many who dedicate time to developing awareness and publishing research helping others to develop techniques for communicating with spirit through electronic instruments. The Association of Transcommunication uses the phrase *instrumental trans-communication* which is now widely accepted term for receiving communications on all different types of electronic devices including TV's, fax machines and phones in fact a whole host of different devices.

How do you achieve communication with spirit via electronic devices? The following is taken from the Association of trans-communication and offers a starting point for anyone interested in experimenting themselves. It is important to remember that initially the voices may be very quiet and difficult to understand, if at all you are successful. Furthermore it is important to remember that recordings are often only two to four words in length and likely to be faster than expected, thus developing techniques to understand and interpret the voices may take some time.

Recordings can be captured using a simple electronic voice recorder and the background sound produced by the inside mechanical device which the spirit entities can use to from words and sounds. Remember spirits are energy and no longer have voice boxes to form words as you or I would, thus in the background helps this process, as other good background noise would be running water or an ordinary house fan.

Scheduling:-
It is important to sit on a regular basis roughly at the same time of day so spirit can prepare prior to the sitting in order for them to communicate. Try and find somewhere that allows you to be calm and focused on your intentions and also optimises the opportunity for recording voices.

Preparation:-
The site recommends meditating prior to attempting recordings as this enables you to relax and become more focused. I would argue in any situation whereby you are attempting to link with spirit it is important to have a calm mind which is not cluttered by emotions and the day's baggage of work or the stresses of everyday life. If you meditate on a daily basis it is worth offering a thought out to spirit the day before the recording informing them of your intentions to practice EVP. It is also pertinent to offer out a pray to spirit asking only highest spirit to communicate and offer evidence of survival, there's nothing wrong with asking for deceased family members to communicate and offer guidance and protection.

Recording:-
When recording it is important to ask questions out loud and then wait for a period of time for a response (up to ten seconds), and don't forget to ask at the end of the recording if the spirit entity has anything to say, enabling them to potential impart further information. Don't be put off if you don't hear a response, often the voices are picked up when listening back to the recording. When you start to pick up voices often they are strongest at the beginning and may begin prior to asking question so it is important to wait a couple of seconds before speaking just in case. Interestingly many practitioners use to recording devices one which appears to pick up the voices and the other which remains blank except for the sounds and questions asked by yourself.

Playback:-
There seems to be a misconception amongst the wider public that because a spirit personality has passed that they suddenly have the ability to do everything and anything, when in fact it is likely to be as much of a learning experience for them as it is for you! It is perhaps pertinent when trying to communicate with a specific individual in spirit, ways they would have communicated when on the earth plain. Think about how they would have learnt, did they like to write things down to remember? If so write questions for them and leave them in the room a few days before? Was the person a stickler for being organised and on time? Then make sure you are organised and timely for each of your sessions.

Remember that listening to EVP's is a learnt experiences and it may take up to thirty minutes to listen to a three or four minute recording. Also try to keep you sessions short, bearing in mind that spirit are drawing on energy, the sounds around you to communicate efficiently. Finally remember to keep a relatively detailed log of your recordings, as this enables you to track messages and ascertain if there is a theme or pattern to the messages being conveyed. Furthermore recording the length of time, the weather status, your own state of mind will help over time ascertain the optimum conditions for achieving results.

Reflecting on what is required to achieve results, it is interesting to note that it takes self-discipline, time and patient, something which is required in any attempt to build a link with spirit! A more detailed description of developing EVP techniques can be found on the Association of Trans-communication website, which the above brief synopsis taken from.

There are many scientists and academics who have an interest in EVP recording, one being Alexandra Mcrae an electronics engineer who worked communication systems for space shuttles at Nasa. Alexandra Mcrae has been investigating EVP for decades, initially sceptical of the phenomenon he has since gone on to become a strong advocate and continues to study the work to this day. Sceptics will often state that EVP is nothing more than misinterpreted radio transmissions picked up on the recording devices used, yet despite this Alexandra has run experiments in a laboratory under test conditions. This enabled him to test the paranormal nature of the voices, ruling out the argument that the voices are nothing more than misinterpreted natural phenomenon or that of radio wave transmissions. Remarkable the voices still were recorded and in one, a voice can be heard saying: *'be a voyager'*.

Evidence from Medical Professionals: Chapter eleven

For years there have been reports from medical professionals claiming to have witnessed paranormal experiences when working with critically unwell patients. Often these professionals and nurses keep their experiences to themselves fearing ridicule and judgement of their professional capability. I recall when at university a bright young lady called Hannah asked me about mediumship and some of my experiences. Hannah described some of the visits she had from her grandfather from beyond the grave and it was clear that she was a naturally gifted medium. Concerned for her wellbeing and sanity Hannah told me that she had been to see her GP about her experiences who told her she had mental health issues! How sad that rather than exploring these experiences further, he chose to tell her she was mentally unwell and ultimately try to prescribe medication for this.

In this section I want to highlight some of the research and experiences of these individuals, whilst also looking at the patient's experiences including near death experiences, out of body experiences and how these have impacted on their life.

Nurses work with critically unwell individuals on a daily basis, often in tough conditions and underpaid for the hard work they do. Arguably nurses see us at our most vulnerable, when we are on the cusp of our current world and ready to take the transition to the next. Given that hospitals are a place where many people die, it's not surprising that many report ghostly type experiences. I recall sitting with my Auntie watching my Grandmother slowly pass away, whilst in hospital. Whilst laid there I became aware of a spirit personality stood near the side of her bed and noticed my Grandmother start to mumble, try to sit up and reach out to someone. My Grandma passed away a few days later, yet I was comforted knowing that someone was waiting to greet her on the other side.

Nurses often report such incidents, witnessing ill individuals calling out to unseen persons, or just before they pass seeing them smile and talk to unseen persons in the room. There are stories from medical professionals of feeling a sense of peace surrounding someone just before they die and a comforting feeling encompasses the room. Some nurses report patients who talk about visiting the afterlife briefly and then coming back to pass messages on to relatives or enabling them to deal with a specific issue before they transition.

There are stories from nurses who state they see the soul leaving the body, or feel it passing in the room when the patient's life comes to an end. It is not uncommon for nurses to describe seeing brilliant white/golden light leaving the body too. Whilst anecdotal evidence, there are numerous first-hand accounts from palliative nurses discussing their experiences when caring for individual's in the last stages of their life. Nurses are professionals, taught to be critical and medical in their knowledge and perspectives on death; often they are articulate and intellectual and it would be foolish to disregard their experiences.

Near death experiences:

Near death experience's (NDE's) are a unique type of evidence for survival after death, in part because they offer us a glimpse of what happens when we pass over in the initial stages; but also because they throw up questions about our current understanding of how the mind works. From the current medical perspective NDE'S are no more than a lack of oxygen and blood to the brain which causes tunnel like vision and tricking the mind into thinking your experiencing a spiritual vision. The argument is further supported by studies which indicate with the right stimulation to certain parts of the brain this can trigger similar experiences such as euphoria and a sense of leaving the body.

It is important to try and understand any spiritual experience using the current understanding of how the mind works, and a natural explanation for NDE's is further underpinned by the experiences of sleep paralysis. This is where individuals wake up in the night and feel paralysed and a sense of someone watching you. I recently experienced this for the first time myself whilst having a disrupted sleep pattern. I woke in the early hours of the morning and felt as though there was a figure in the doorway and I was unable to move my body or my head. Sleep paralysis is not uncommon and I am sure for anyone that experiences them they can be frightening and scary. I was recently asked if I could visit a property and work out if it was haunted following the owners recent strange experience. When they explained what had been occurring I immediately notice the familiar pattern of sleep paralysis, which included waking with a sense of someone in the room and not being able to move her body and a sense of fear. I find it interesting when explaining this was not paranormal in nature but sleep paralysis; rather than accepting this as a logical explanation, the individual chose to continue to believe this was a spiritual experience. It is really important to distinguish psychological phenomenon and spiritual experiences, ensuring that people have a greater awareness of what is in the mind and natural normal experiences.

I recall going to watch a self-trained psychic a number of years ago and during the interval, a lady came up to him and told him of an experiences similar to the above and wanted help and guidance. I was just about to explain to her about sleep paralysis and to my horror the self-trained psychic told her it was demon trying to possess her! Imagine my horror and the look of horror on the poor women's face, luckily I was able to intervene and explain it was a natural occurrence and nothing to worry about. I do get concerned about how vulnerable sitters can be in instances such as this; and how many of them are left to deal with the fear that a suppose demon could be waiting for them on their return home. If you do ever experience sleep paralysis, the advice for people is to try and wiggle your fingers and this should kick your brain into gear and reset your sleep pattern. Essentially Sleep paralysis is the mind trying to make sense when in between the different sleep stages and this is why these experiences happen. If you are concerned or experience regular episodes of sleep paralysis you are much safer going to your doctor than to the local spiritualist church. Finally I thought it would be beneficial to highlight that some individuals who regularly misuse Ketamine, a horse tranquilliser who report experiencing similar experiences to those who have been near the end of their lives. This adds weight to scientific theories that near death experiences are nothing more than chemical changes in the brain causing hallucinations and altered states of consciousness.

Can all these experiences be put down to a lack of oxygen to the brain, or equally hallucinations when an individual is pumped full of medicine to sustain their life in times of crisis? Advocates who study NDE's and believe they are more than the mind playing tricks argue that the vivid nature and clarity during these experiences is not how the brain would act, when starved of oxygen and blood. Rather they argue that the images would be confused blurry and not logical in nature. To add further wait to the argument for NDE's often the experiences following a specific pattern, which is consistent regardless of your cultural background. There are many articles regarding NDE's and experiments carried out by medical professionals both arguing for and against such phenomenon.

What are the common themes?

Noted NDE researcher P.M.H. Atwater has catalogued many of the common themes in a "Common Aspects Analysis", and Kevin Williams has further analysed them based on an examination of 50 NDEs profiled on the Near-Death Experiences and the Afterlife website.

A tunnel/Bright Light – Probably the most common experiences between all NDE's is the idea of the soul leaving the body, often in a lifting sensation, travelling through a tunnel, usually with a bright light which is intensives but does not blind them. This experience is sometimes described as seeing a staircase and a door, or other sensations of having to make a transition like crossing a river, which perhaps is symbolic of the transition between this world and the next.

A feeling of overwhelming contentment and love – often people who have experienced NDE's described an encompassing feeling on love, either that from an unknown but all seeing force, or from light beings they are greeted by. Sometimes people describe this feeling as the love of God, or other deities associated with their own faiths.

Mental Telepathy – a vast majority of NDE's experiences describe a sense of meeting with other beings and instantly knowing information. This suggests that communication happens on a nonphysical level through the connectedness of consciousness. Tied with this, is a feeling of a greater depth of knowledge, whether that be having a greater understanding of life or understanding information in greater detail. For me this is an interesting component of Near Death Experiences as it ties in strongly with information past of from spirits during direct voice communication or physical mediumship demonstrations.

Life Review – Arguably the most well-known part of NDE's and something which is common knowledge in the mainstream media and public conscious. No doubt you would have heard of people talking about their life flashing before their eyes when experiencing an accident or freak event. In the context of NDE's, this experience is deeper, more profound and usually consists of the individual reviewing their life without the restraints of time we would experience on earth. Similar to telepathy it would appear that we can review our life in an instance, being able to see it all at once. Usually the life review involves some reflection on your life so far and the impact your decisions have had both on yourself and others. This process isn't a negative one, nor to make you feel sad, it is about learning and understanding yourself and how these events have shaped you as an individual. This process sometimes is described with other spirit beings supporting you through or by reflecting on your life with a higher sentient being.

Tremendous Ecstasy – This feeling closely links to the feeling on all encompassing love, but is slightly different in its description. Rather than an external feeling of love, this feeling comes from within and comes from not being constrained by earthly emotions such as jealousy, anger and anxiety. This feeling is accompanied by a feeling of contentment being surrounding by passed family members and other spiritual beings.

Unlimited Knowledge – Often upon their return individuals state they felt connected to a presence of unlimited knowledge, stating that they have a greater understanding of their place and meaning of life. It is interesting to note that these individuals do not immediately have the ability to do everything, but they are able to begin accessing this information if required. Reports indicate that whilst individuals experience this, they do not retain this information upon their recovery; yet these experiences have a profound impact on how they choose to live their life.

Afterlife Levels – As with communications from spirit through physical mediums, Individual's experiencing NDE's talk about multi layered levels or realms within the spirit world. It is perhaps worth mentioning that some individuals experience worlds which are not calm or tranquil where some souls reside who still have learning to do from their lives when living in here on Earth. Personally I am not sure how I feel about this, perhaps this is where souls reside until they are ready to grow, learn and love compassionately. Regardless it is safe to say these experiences have a life changing and profound impact on the said individuals who experience them.

Being told it times to go back – Obviously individuals who pass over to spirit and return it is clear that they are not ready to make the transition to spirit. Often people state they have travelled through a bright light tunnel, and then meet up with spirit family on the other side. At this point often individuals are advised it is not their time and encouraged to come back, or alternatively their mission is not complete. This idea that a mission is not complete is interesting as it would suggest that prior to coming to Earth we have certain events which we need to experience to enable the soul to grow. Many NDE individual's state they have been reluctant to return, wanting to remain where they are but this decision is not made by them and they are guided back to their earthly existence.

A debate without resolution – the final common theme between all NDE's is their belief that these events where real, even when materialist scientists offer perceived rational experiences such as the medical opinion. Whilst we cannot rule out fully that these experiences are not explained away by normal rational means, the fact these events are usually life changing and so vivid for the people that experiencing them, coupled with the fact that the stories are so consistent they warrant further exploration.

Although slightly different, Out of body experiences sometimes happen to individuals who are receiving treatment following trauma.

Some individuals state that they see leave their body and see themselves laid on the bed or operating table whilst medical professionals operate on them. Like NDE's, Out of body experiences have similar feelings of contentment and a sense of peace. I mention this because there have been serious reviews into NDE's and OBE's within medical settings to try and ascertain a better understanding of these experiences. Included within this, are experiments such as hiding a random object in the room which can only been seen when having a supposed out of body experiences or near death experience.

Scientific evidence

I recently came across an article in the Telegraph newspaper from Southampton University published in 2004. At the time, it was the largest ever medical study into near death experiences and out of body experiences and discovered that *some awareness may continue* even after the brain has shut down completely. So what does this mean? In the current scientific paradigm, death of the individual is classed as the brain stem function stops. This happens through lack of oxygen and lack of blood flow quickly leading to permanent loss of brain stem function. Whilst an individual may be kept 'alive' through the use of ventilators to pump blood through the heart, essentially the loss of function within the brain stem means that consciousness no longer continues. Therefore in a medical context when this functions stops, consciousness stops and the individual no longer exists.

Yet the study conducted by Southampton University which spent four years examining more than 2,000 people who suffered cardiac arrests at 15 hospitals in the UK, US and Australia discovered something interesting. The scientist found that nearly forty per cent of people who survived, experienced some kind of 'awareness' when they were 'clinically dead', before the heart was restarted. One man even recalled leaving his body completely and watching medical practitioners attempting to resuscitate him whilst he watched from the corner of the room. Despite being unconscious and in a medical context 'dead', the 57 year old Social Worker recounted the actions of the nursing staff in detail and described the sounds of the machines operating in the room.

The article goes on to reference Dr Sam Parnia, a former research fellow at Southampton University, now at the state of University of New York who led the study: -

'We know the brain can't function when the heart stops beating, but in this case conscious awareness appears to have continued for up to three minutes into the period when the heart wasn't beating. Even though the brain typically shuts down within 20 – 30 seconds after the heart has stopped. The man described everything that had happened in the room, but importantly, he heard two bleeps from a machine that makes noises at three minutes intervals. So we could time how long the experienced lasted for. He seemed very credible and everything that he said had happened to him had actually happened.'

Of 2,060 cardiac arrest patients studied, 330 survived and of 140 surveyed, 39 per cent said they experienced some kind of awareness during the period they were being resuscitated. During the study, there were many who could not recall specific details, however common themes did emerge. One in five stated they felt an unusual sense of peacefulness while nearly one third said time had slowed down or sped up. Some individuals recalled seeing a bright light; a golden flash or the sun shining. Others recounted feelings of fear or drowning or being dragged through deep water, whilst 13 per cent said they felt separated from their bodies and the same number experienced heightened senses.

Dr Parnia believes that many more may have experienced similar experiences when close to death but drugs or sedatives used in the process of trying to save individuals lives may impact on their ability to recall experiences. Dr Parnia continues by stating:-

'Estimates have suggested that millions of people have had vivid experiences in relation to death but scientific evidence has been ambiguous at best. Many people have assumed that these were hallucinations or illusions but they do seem to correspond to actual events. These experiences warrant further investigation. Most studies look retrospectively, 10 or 20 years ago, but the researchers went out looking for examples and used a really large sample size, so this gives the research a lot of validity. There is some good evidence here

that these experiences are actually happening after people have medically died. We just don't know what is going on. We are still very much in the dark about what happens when you die and hopefully this study will help shine a scientific lens onto that.'

You can find the full article for this in the Telegraph, science, published by Sarah Knapton, 07th October 2014. The Study was published in the Resuscitation journal.

There are numerous studies which can be accessed regarding these specific types of experiences. What is important about such studies is that it takes anecdotal evidence from individuals and puts it in a scientific paradigm, enabling these to be collectively peer reviewed by the scientific community. It is also interesting to note, that the experiences described by individuals who have passed when communicating through mediums, correlate with the experiences published within the study, thus further building the case for survival after death.

It is often said that the human brain is the most complex thing known to man, not only on earth but throughout the universe. Whilst some scientist may believe that consciousness is nothing more than an illusion, the above study suggests that there is more to this than once thought. I would love to discuss in detail the possible links between consciousness and quantum physics, including superposition states, however it is difficult to articulate in simple terms and in honesty difficult for me to understand. Despite my lack of ability to explain quantum physics simply, the idea that there is a connection between consciousness and quantum physics continues to be studied by physicist, as it was by the early pioneers in the early 20th century. I would be foolish in writing that I believe quantum mechanics can explain mediumship or experiences such as poltergeist phenomenon. When in fact due to spiritualists and mystical teachings using the idea of quantum physics in skewed way has ultimately led to many scientists being reluctant to explore the subject in an open forum for fear of ridicule. But the very fact it is a genuine area of interest for physicist again argues for a better medical understanding of death and what happens to the conscious mind once we past.

Teachings from the spirit world:
Chapter Twelve

In this final chapter I want to take a look at what the spirit world is trying to teach and why they on the other side choice to make contact with us to demonstrate survival after death. I can honestly say in the years I have been undertaking mediumship I have not come across anything evil or negative, despite the portrayed media and supposed 'Americanised paranormal type of investigations'. Communication with spirit is more than that, at its simplest it is to heal and bring comfort to the bereaved. Whilst at its deepest it's about connecting to something bigger which enables you to grow as an individual both here in the physical form and on a deeper spiritual level.

There is a famous phrase from the Bible (John14:2) which states:- *'My Father's house has many rooms; if that were not so, would I have told you that I am going to prepare a place for you?*

Arguably this quote could be perceived to embrace all religions, recognising that there are many threads and themes to interpret a higher force. Sadly we live in a world whereby religion is often governed by human emotions and is used to dictate, control and influence people for either individual gain or to progress the power of said religion. Yet at the core of every religious teaching there is a common theme about self-development, respect for others and a greater sense of self and peace. It is not just the main religions where emotions influence and impact on the greater good. Sadly this occurs in the spiritual movement to, either through jealousies or the need to control and gain a greater position of power. As with every religion, in Spiritualism there are those who give of themselves wholly and strive to uphold the underpinning values that they believe in. Margaret West who I dedicate this book to, is one such lady who for many years gave much of her life to the local Spiritualist Church in

Grimsby, welcoming new persons and also ensuring that the church remained open.

Although not direct messages from spirit, the above is important because it demonstrates the need to remove the ego from one's self and strive to be a better person. Don't get me wrong there are times when my emotions have got the better of me and I have either become frustrated towards others or alternatively become jealous. I am sure this happens with other genuine mediums but the difference is that you recognise it, see it has an opportunity to develop the self-further, grow and learn.

I genuinely believe there is a misconception amongst most people purporting to be linked to spirit stating their guides give direct teachings and speak to them on a daily basis. Usually these are the people whose messages and content are often poor and it's more about their ego rather than teachings from spirit. Whilst there are people who do hear their guides speak to them, usually these are mediums who have dedicated many years to developing that link, rather than 6 months in a development group. My guides do give me teachings, often subtle hints which I am expected to interpret or alternatively meditate on and utilise in everyday life. What would be the point of them just giving a teaching, we learn better when we strive to find truth ourselves or experience something tangible which we then can reflect on? For me it is a fine balance between trying to develop on a deeper spiritual level and using my life experience to help me grow spiritually too. It is not healthy to try and live your life 'spiritualised' as whilst spirit are there to guide us, ultimately our lessons and spiritual growth come from our own life experiences, whether they be happy, sad or in-between, our everyday life is where we grow!

Things I have learnt about the spirit world since doing readings:

Over the year I have learnt much about the spirit world, its workings, how spirit attempt to interact with us and make their presence known. I have also had some insight into what occurs after we die and how we continue to develop and change. There appears to be a misconception amongst some that when we pass over we live in a world whereby we stay the same for eternity but that is misleading and what purpose would that serve? I regularly give readings where I bring an individual through and they present how they did in life, with the same personalities whether they were jovial, anger or quiet. They do this for one simple reason and that is because if they came through enlightened and changed then they wouldn't be providing evidence of who they were when on the earth plain. I recently did a reading where a father figure came through who was a drunk, aggressive and violent towards his daughter, the person I was reading for. The sitter's brother came through as well, who throughout his life was a drug user, an alcohol user and led a life with regular involvement from the Police. It was clear from the sitter's face that this information struck a core with her on an emotional level. By providing this detail I was able to demonstrate their survival and personality; but I was then able to touch on how these life experiences shaped them and enabled them to grow and change once in spirit.

My understanding of the spirit world is that it consists of different levels which individuals progress through as they learn and let go of their earthly feelings overtime. There are many writings about the spirit world describing it has a world of thought, which to a degree is created by the individual spirit. In the teachings which spirit bought through Leslie Flint suggest that initially once passed spirits enter a world much like our own. They continue to have a body, continue to have earthly desires such as cravings for food, or other earthly creations. As the individual spirit learns to become accustom to their new surroundings they start to become less attached to their earthly ways. As part of this process they reflect on their life experiences and begin to understand how they have grown in a spiritual context.

There are also teachings from spirit which indicate as the individual comes into context with other spirits they experience new teachings which in turn helps them to learn and understand more on a deeper level. Going back to the reading I recently gave, the two individuals who came through would have been on different levels in the spirit, most probably past those initial stages, but by coming back how they were in life enabled them to provide evidence and in turn then demonstrate how they have changed and want the opportunity to apologise for how they acted on earth.

My understanding that these different levels in spirit are countless and probably overlap on some levels, but it is clear from spirit teachings that they continue to grow, learn and gain a greater sense of the true meaning of life. During the Scole Experiment the spirit personalities spoke about having to learn how to develop skills in order to produce phenomenon such as produce pictures on films or alternatively demonstrate evidence of items lifting, or spirits showing themselves in the room. This is equally true for spirit guides working with a medium on mental level, they have to learn and understand how to communicate with you, and this is partly why it takes many years to build that link.

Taking this back to a spirit who might be trying to communicate during a reading, it may be their first attempt and they might find it difficult. Add in the mind-set of the sitter/medium and the medium's own skills it can become a complex business trying to get a message across. It is not surprising I often find that people I would have got on well with in life, I find it easier to communicate with them.

Overtime as spirit individuals learn more and adapt to their new surroundings they no longer require the use of a body, as the world of spirit is thought and the need for a physical identity becomes less important. What remains is the essence of the individual, their soul with their earthly memories and life experiences. Personally I am not fully sure whether reincarnation is something which occurs, or if this is open to every individual but it would make sense if the soul's journey is about continually growth and self-development. Having different lives enables you to experience different perspectives and challenges which when returning to the spirit world enables you to grow some more. Whilst I do not believe in the concept of hell, I do think it is worth pondering if the lives we live on earth are the hardest experiences we go through as souls, perhaps this is the most difficult experiences we go through in all. The above description of many levels of growth and development is still a basic interpretation but it is difficult to fully express what the spirit world actually is. I would be foolish to write that I have a detailed understanding of the spirit world, as during the years all I have experienced is brief glimpses of what it available to us once we pass on.

In our western culture death has become something we fear, an event which becomes so profound and difficult to live with. Whilst sad, in reality death is part of life, part of natural selection which affects every living being on Earth, whether that is the tiny ant or our family. Often in readings I come across people who have lost their way or become anger carrying that grief throughout their life for many years afterwards. I see people focussed on the way the person died, the trauma and tragedy surrounding it and this has a profound impact on their emotions. I do not want to minimise the impact of losing someone, especially those who have gone too early or died in tragic circumstances, those who leave our lives are more than just how they died. During readings I always try and bring memories back, happy memories as part of the process for healing people. Gordon Smith the great Scottish medium talks about Jewels of the mind, those memories which we can link to, to reconnect with that person and remember the happy and profound impact they had on our lives. This is such an important part of delivering messages to the bereaved, helping them move from a mind-set of anger and despair to a place of happiness and contentment.

Suicide

I want to touch on the subject of suicide, arguably one of the most traumatic experiences an individual, their family and friends go through. Sadly some religions teach that these individuals are punished after death, experiencing years in purgatory for taking their own life which is against the religious dogma. I have read for people who have experienced such tragedies and my own experience is that they do not enter purgatory, more they receive healing upon returning to spirit. They are given help and taught about how their actions have affected and impacted others. So often these individuals come through emotional initially wanting to show remorse but also let their families know they are safe.

Final thoughts

Writing this book has been a little journey in itself, and I have come to realise how much I have learnt in the last decade or more. Mediumship and spiritual development has had such a profound impact on my life, in such a positive way. It has allowed me to have a better understanding of myself, the world around me and what happens after death. It has also enabled me to have a better understanding of my own values and the type of mediumship I so desperately what to strive towards. Developing spiritually and practising mediumship does not mean that I am special, nor better than any other person, but it has made me realise what can be achieved through hard work, trust and patience.

I hope this book has helped the reader develop a greater understanding of the mechanics of mediumship, its purpose and ultimately what you should expect when having a reading with a medium/psychic. The topics discussed particularly in the latter sections are areas of mediumship so often ignored by the mainstream media and by many scientists alike, yet they offer strong evidence for the survival of the conscious mind which is presently outside our understanding of the natural world. I am genuinely passionate about honest and ethical mediumship away from the pantomime psychics and mediums so many of us come across. To quote David Fontana, Psychologist, past President of the Society for Psychical Research and Chair of the Survival Research Committee:

'Mediumship, like so many human abilities appears to be more of an art than a science. And in all areas, great artists are few and far between. (9.2005)

Mediumship cannot always be tested in strict scientific conditions, yet through data analysis, good observation and work with spirit teams, results can be achieved. It is so important for links to be developed further between universities, academics and genuine mediums to explore these human abilities and to ascertain and understand what lies beyond death. There is perhaps a paradox with this idea though, and worth reflecting on why it has been difficult to prove survival after death? Perhaps in the greater scheme of things, as a collective consciousness we are not ready to understand such information and the likely impact this would have on the world.

I hope this book has given you an idea of what being a medium is like and what information is available both in English speaking countries and abroad. I hope it gives you a platform to explore survival after death in an informed and ethically manner. There are so many subjects in this book which I have not touched on, partly due to space, partly due to my own need to explore further and perhaps will be discussed in future books! Who knows! I end this book with my warmest regards, love and light, Mediumjoe xx

About the author

Joe Haigh lives in Barton upon Humber a village near the Humber Bridge in Northern Lincolnshire. Having always been fascinated with Ghostbusters and stories of ghost throughout his life, this was ignited when visiting a local medium and being told he was gifted and would be communicating with spirit on church rostrums in five years, this later proved to be correct. Following a stuttering career as a Mechanic, Joe changed careers in 2007 studying Social Work at Lincoln University, qualifying with a first class honours degree and then going on to get multiple post graduate qualifications including successfully training as an Approved Mental Health Practitioner. Joe now combines his knowledge of Spiritualism and his scientific training to demonstrate mediumship in and around the Lincolnshire area, raising over £3,000 pounds different charities in the process. Joe currently works as a mental health professional in the Grimsby area has three children and two chocolate Labradors.

Printed in Great Britain
by Amazon